THE **COMPLETE IDIOT'S GUIDE**® TO

Leadership

FAST-TRACK

by Susan Caba

ALPHA

A member of Penguin Group (USA) Inc.

ALPHA BOOKS

Published by Penguin Group (USA) Inc.

Penguin Group (USA) Inc., 375 Hudson Street, New York, New York 10014, USA • Penguin Group (Canada), 90 Eglinton Avenue East, Suite 700, Toronto, Ontario M4P 2Y3, Canada (a division of Pearson Penguin Canada Inc.) • Penguin Books Ltd., 80 Strand, London WC2R 0RL, England • Penguin Ireland, 25 St. Stephen's Green, Dublin 2, Ireland (a division of Penguin Books Ltd.) • Penguin Group (Australia), 250 Camberwell Road, Camberwell, Victoria 3124, Australia (a division of Pearson Australia Group Pty. Ltd.) • Penguin Books India Pvt. Ltd., 11 Community Centre, Panchsheel Park, New Delhi—110 017, India • Penguin Group (NZ), 67 Apollo Drive, Rosedale, North Shore, Auckland 1311, New Zealand (a division of Pearson New Zealand Ltd.) • Penguin Books (South Africa) (Pty.) Ltd., 24 Sturdee Avenue, Rosebank, Johannesburg 2196, South Africa • Penguin Books Ltd., Registered Offices: 80 Strand, London WC2R 0RL, England

Copyright © 2013 by Penguin Group (USA), Inc.

International Standard Book Number: 978-1-61564-242-7
Library of Congress Catalog Card Number: 2012947177

15 14   8 7 6 5 4 3

Interpretation of the printing code: The rightmost number of the first series of numbers is the year of the book's printing; the rightmost number of the second series of numbers is the number of the book's printing. For example, a printing code of 13-1 shows that the first printing occurred in 2013.

Printed in the United States of America

Note: This publication contains the opinions and ideas of its author. It is intended to provide helpful and informative material on the subject matter covered. It is sold with the understanding that the author and publisher are not engaged in rendering professional services in the book. If the reader requires personal assistance or advice, a competent professional should be consulted.

The author and publisher specifically disclaim any responsibility for any liability, loss, or risk, personal or otherwise, which is incurred as a consequence, directly or indirectly, of the use and application of any of the contents of this book.

Publisher: *Mike Sanders*
Executive Managing Editor: *Billy Fields*
Senior Acquisitions Editor: *Tom Stevens*
Development Editor: *Jennifer Moore*
Senior Production Editor: *Kayla Dugger*
Copy Editor: *Louise Lund*

Cover Designer: *Kurt Owens*
Book Designers: *William Thomas, Rebecca Batchelor*
Indexer: *Angie Martin*
Layout: *Ayanna Lacey*
Proofreader: *Amy Lepore*

To my son, Max Banerjee, who inspires me to have faith in the leaders of the future.

Contents

1 Leadership: The Buck Stops Here 1

Focusing on Values, Vision, and Mission 2

Walking the Talk 4

A Wink, a Nod, and a Salute..*5*

Fair Is Fair *6*

Measurable Results Mount *7*

Developing Relationships 7

Admitting Mistakes...8

Leadership Lessons Served with Popcorn..........................9

2 Leader, Know Thyself!... **11**

Getting a Grip on Personality Types 12

Restless Drivers: Task-Oriented Extroverts *14*

Social Influencers: People-Focused Extroverts...............*15*

Steady Eddies: People-Focused Introverts........................*16*

Compliant Analytics: Task-Focused Introverts................*17*

Bridging the Gaps Between Personality Types..................18

Deciphering Messages *19*

Communicating with Different Personalities................... *20*

Putting Communication Strategies to Work....................21

Restless Driver: Take Early Action................................*22*

Social Influencer: Curb Your Compassion *22*

Steady Eddie: Face Up to Conflict................................*24*

Compliant Analytic: Call for Backup *25*

Which Style Is Best? 26

3 Communication: More Than Just Talk.......................... **29**

Developing a Communication Strategy ..,........................30

Strategic Communication Is an Effective Tool *30*

Nine Principles of Strategic Communication *31*

Cultural Awareness 32

Know Your Audience...*33*

Buy-In Begins at the Beginning *34*

Who Carries Out Your Communication Strategy?...........34

The Executive Team...*35*

Supervisors *35*

The Rank-and-File *35*

Leaders Communicate Authenticity, Clarity, and
　Direction 36
　　Making a Personal Commitment to Your Cause...............*37*
　　Loosen Up a Little...*37*
Everybody Loves Face Time! 38
Supervisors Possess Credibility as Your Surrogate............39
Communication Is a Call-and-Response Activity 40
　　Getting Feedback from Your Employees............................*41*
　　Accepting Criticism Graciously....................................*42*
Leaders No Longer Have All the Answers—or Control ...43
Tips for Active Listening....................................... 44

4　Getting Eggs to Fly: Facilitating Change 47
Get Your Ducks in a Row...................................... 48
Keep Your Friends Close and Your Enemies Closer 48
　　How Much Difference Can One Person Make? *49*
　　Embrace Your Opposition *50*
Change Behavior to Change Attitudes.........................51
　　Achieve Multiple Goals with a Single Strategy.................*52*
　　Reward the Results You Value Most...............................*53*
How Do You Eat an Elephant? 54
Make the Most of Your Existing Resources.........................56
　　Substitute Creativity When Money Is Short *56*
　　Reassess and Reassign Your Assets...............................*57*

5　Hire Good People 59
Creating a Culture of Constant Recruitment................... 60
　　Keep Your Pipeline Primed.....................................*60*
　　Turn Your Employees into Talent Scouts *62*
　　Put Your Brand to Work......................................*63*
　　Identify Your Prime Hunting Grounds *64*
　　Harness Facebook, YouTube, and More *65*
Hiring for Diversity... 66
Staying in Touch *67*
Screening Candidates... 68
　　Require References and Check 'Em! *69*
　　Prehire Testing...*70*

Preparing for the Interview..71
Checking Core Competencies...72
On-Boarding New Employees 73

6 Work That Matters.. **77**
Meaning Is in the Mind of the Beholder...........................78
Employee Engagement Is an Emotional Bond...................79
The Difference Between Engagement and Motivation..... 80
To Motivate or Engage? 80
Responsibility Lightens the Load...81
Input Multiplies Commitment Fivefold...........................82
Advancement + Growth = Achievement 83
This "Drug" Has No Bad Effects.......................................83
Give Praise in a Language the Recipient "Gets"...............85
Taking the Pulse of Employee Engagement 86
Work and Well-Being Survey...87
Engaged Employees Make Your Business Better................89

7 Lead 'Em, Don't Assault 'Em!.. **91**
Setting the Tone for Mutual Respect................................92
Positive Leaders Are Okay with Loose Reins of
Control 93
Create a Positive Atmosphere for Growing Success 94
Accomplishing Change Is Easier in a Positive Climate.....94
Positive Leaders Adapt in a Crisis.....................................96
P.S.: Sometimes It's Okay to Be Authoritarian 96
Focusing on Strengths, Not Weaknesses, Enhances
Success 97
Does Everyone—or Anyone—Recognize Their
Strengths?..98
Satisfaction Is Rooted in Expertise and Achievement 98
Enrich Jobs by Adding More Challenging Tasks 99
Everyone Benefits When an Employee's Expertise
Grows 100
Reward Increased Ability with More Responsibility.........100
Money Isn't Everything, If You Have Enough to Live 101

8 You Can Fail But Still Prevail................................**103**

Adaptability and Laser Focus on Goals Save a
Doomed Crew 104

Mistakes Teach Great Lessons, If You're Willing
to Learn 105

Expecting Perfection Sets the Stage for Failure *105*

Respond Compassionately to Honest Mistakes *106*

Acknowledging Failure Is a Strength 107

Put Your Organization First...108

Three Strategies for Ensuring Spectacular Failure 109

Dirt Under the Rug Always Rises to the Surface *110*

Why Are You All Picking On Me?....................................*110*

*The Dark Side of Leadership: Company Culture
Decays*...*112*

*Employees Are Obliged to Stop a Leader Who
Causes Harm* *113*

9 Building Team Leadership at Every Level **115**

A Team Isn't Just a Group of People Working
Together 116

Teams Are More Than the Sum of Their Parts 117

Bringing Harmony to Your C-Suite Team 118

*Assembling Your Team Based on Complementary
Abilities* *118*

Developing and Managing Your Executive Team *119*

A Dysfunctional Team Can Produce Sour Results *120*

Creating a Company-Wide Team-Based Structure...........120

Tap Your Organization's Informal Teams........................122

Harley-Davidson Test-Drives Team Leadership 123

10 Developing Leaders of the Future **125**

Act Now! Avoid the Coming Leadership Crisis................126

Create a Diverse Portfolio of Emerging Talent................*127*

High-Potential Candidates Are Like Gold.......................*127*

Helping High Achievers Reach Their Potential 128
   Aha! Moments: Develop Your Capacity for
     Adaptive Thinking *129*
   Making Succession Planning a Priority *130*
   Five Must-Have Qualities for Leaders *131*
   Involve the Board *132*
Mentoring Rising Stars 132
Developing the Soft Skills 133

Index **135**

Introduction

There are literally thousands of books and articles written about leadership. They boil down to about six basic principles. Put them in practice, and you're on your way to becoming a leader. If you continue to study great leaders, you'll refine your own leadership style and, possibly, become great yourself.

Regardless of the type of organization they work for, effective leaders follow the same principles and practices. Even the Mafia employs leadership best practices—great leaders aren't limited to positive organizations.

The basics are as follows:

- Know your values and live them every day.
- Clearly communicate your goals and standards.
- Be aware of your behavior style and how you interact with others.
- Hire great people, give them challenging work, and then let them do their jobs.
- Manage change, don't force it.
- Create opportunities for people to learn and practice leadership skills at every level.

This book helps you develop these principles and put them in practice.

How This Book Is Organized

The most important characteristic of great leaders is integrity. They know their values and demonstrate them daily. As you'll read in **Chapter 1** and throughout *The Complete Idiot's Guide to Leadership Fast-Track*, great leaders build relationships on a level of trust that develops because their actions match their words.

Leadership is based on relationships. **Chapter 2** explains the four basic behavior types and how they interact with one another. Knowing your own style, as well as those of your colleagues, helps you achieve mutual goals more effectively.

Communication is the foundation of leadership. You need a communication strategy to help drive your mission, and **Chapter 3** discusses how to develop and execute that strategy. Your communication strategy should be inclusive (invite everyone to participate), interactive (listen as well as talk), and authentic (develop real relationships).

Leadership is about managing change. **Chapter 4** covers different strategies to facilitate change, including recruiting allies, focusing resources where they are most needed, and changing behavior to change attitudes.

Great people are vital for leadership success. **Chapters 5, 6,** and **7** cover hiring top people, creating an engaged workforce, and managing through positive—not punitive—measures.

Of course, mistakes will be made and disasters do happen. How you respond as a leader will decide whether your organization learns valuable lessons or suffers irreparable damage. **Chapter 8** focuses on how to prevail in times of adversity.

In our complex global society, leaders rarely work alone. They create teams. Part of **Chapter 9** is about finding the right mix for your executive leadership team. The second segment discusses how to build and encourage leadership teams at every level of your organization.

Finally, the greatest leaders are constantly learning. They look inward as well as outward for lessons. And they consider it their responsibility to create future leaders. That philosophy is the subject of **Chapter 10.**

Extras

I've sprinkled tips, warnings, and definitions throughout the book in sidebars. They look like this:

FOCUS

These leadership tips keep you focused and ready for action.

BREAK POINT

Here you'll find practices likely to undermine your effectiveness as a leader.

DEFINITION

Look to these sidebars for definitions of terms you may not be familiar with.

Acknowledgments

Writing this book brought together several conversational threads I've been having about leadership and motivation over the past many years with a handful of friends.

First and foremost, Jo Anne Myers, founder of Sunstone International Coaching, who is molten intuition—to be able to tap into her lava flow of knowledge is a privilege. She knows leadership from the academic and business perspective. Much more importantly, she is clairvoyant in seeing what motivates people—and what holds them back. She also exemplifies the concept that leaders are always learning; Jo Anne never accepts her own status quo.

Larry Kesslin and Chris Winter, co-authors of *Break Points—A Business Fable: Where Businesses Get Stuck Between 0–100 Employees*, have been helping business people develop their leadership skills and teams for many years. Working with Larry and Chris helped me see how different leadership types interact successfully—or not.

Robert Fox, president of Channel Compass, Inc., is always enthusiastic and supportive. He's great at devising ways to implement change—a leader's job—by building it into the structure of a mission. If you change behavior, eventually a changed attitude follows.

In the journalism world, Fran Dauth is an editor with both excellent insights into content and a deft touch with the word scalpel. It's as though she sprinkles stardust over the words; you know they have more sparkle but you can't say why. Robert Woodward, my professor at Drake University, taught me more about journalism than anyone else (except Dr. Francois). He also gave me the courage to do the things I am afraid to do.

Finally, thanks to Jenny Phipps, Dianne Benson Harrington, and Joan Tharp at Freelance Success, a wonderful resource for writers, and to Marilyn Allen of Allen O'Shea Literary Agency, who persisted in trying to get in touch with me even after her emails went to spam.

Trademarks

All terms mentioned in this book that are known to be or are suspected of being trademarks or service marks have been appropriately capitalized. Alpha Books and Penguin Group (USA) Inc. cannot attest to the accuracy of this information. Use of a term in this book should not be regarded as affecting the validity of any trademark or service mark.

Leadership: The Buck Stops Here

>>> **In This Chapter**

- Discovering traits that make you a leader
- Focusing on your values, vision, and mission
- Admitting your mistakes and learning from your failures

Leadership isn't defined by a job title. Instead, leadership is both a process and a characteristic. As a leader, you provide purpose, direction, and motivation for others to achieve a mutual or organizational goal. Just reaching the goal doesn't make you a good or great leader. It's ultimately up to others to judge whether you have the character traits—as opposed to the mere authority—to induce them to follow your lead.

As a supervisor or boss, you can rely on your position to get things done. People will follow you because they must, at least within the boundaries of your authority. You may even achieve decent results and win the approval of your superiors. Chances are, though, your people won't give you their all-out effort unless you have demonstrated true traits of leadership—traits that have little to do with title and authority.

Rosa Parks, the African American seamstress who sparked the Montgomery Bus Boycott by refusing to move to the back of the bus, was a leader. She had no authority or position, not even any followers. What she did have was the integrity of her belief that she shouldn't have to move. She became a leader and an icon of the Civil Rights movement.

President Harry S. Truman often described himself as "just an ordinary man." Even his wife considered him unqualified to be president, and when he left office, his approval ratings were around 20 percent. Yet Truman is now considered one of the great U.S. presidents. In part, his status as a great leader is due to his willingness to take responsibility for his actions and the actions of those under him. He uttered one of the ultimate in leadership mantras: "The buck stops here."

Focusing on Values, Vision, and Mission

Effective leaders—whether in the military, business, or sports worlds; religious realms; or social activism movements—have the following characteristics in common:

- A vision of their end goal and the drive to get there
- The ability to define and articulate a mission
- Strategic-planning skills to execute their mission
- Aptitude for connecting and communicating with others
- The capacity to influence events, directly or indirectly
- Willingness to admit mistakes and tolerate them in others
- Fortitude to make unpopular decisions
- Core values that guide their actions and decisions

BREAK POINT

The qualities of effective leaders apply whether their values are good or bad. Mahatma Gandhi, the Indian spiritual and political leader who spearheaded a nonviolent revolt against British colonialism, had a vision based on his values, the drive to achieve it, and the power to influence others to follow his lead. Unfortunately, the same can be said of Adolf Hitler.

Although it appears last on the list, the leadership quality of relying on core values to guide actions and decisions is the most important of them all. "The supreme quality for a leader is integrity," said the late President Dwight D. Eisenhower. That single sentence summarizes the essence of leadership. People want to be led by someone who demonstrates—through his or her actions—a system of moral beliefs and *integrity*.

 DEFINITION

Integrity is disciplined observance of the values that guide a person's actions. A person of integrity doesn't violate his or her beliefs about actions that are right or wrong.

When leaders have integrity, they engender trust. Trust, in turn, creates unity and the willingness to work toward a common goal. When you're trustworthy, you're predictable. When you know people's core values, you can pretty well forecast what they might do under certain circumstances.

Integrity breeds loyalty. Hollow words breed cynicism. There may be no more overused and disbelieved corporate sentence than "Our people are our greatest asset," especially when organizations justify cutting thousands of jobs and employee benefits with the phrase "in the best interest of shareholders."

A blogger, an IT professional who lost his job, quoted his company's website regarding its workers:

> "Who you are matters as much as what you do …. We value our employees as individuals and believe that giving each person the opportunity to succeed is key to achieving our overall corporate goals."

"How timely," wrote the blogger. "I received this the very day I was … told that, because of the ongoing 'restructuring' for our IPO (initial public offering), my position has been eliminated.

The engineering manager just shrugged his shoulders and said that's the way it is."

Leaders who consider employees their greatest assets live up to those words when layoffs are required. They don't deliver the news with a shrug or by email—or worse, phone message— or without an adequate explanation of why terminations are required.

Contrast the IT professional's story with this blog entry from a woman whose company also claims that its people are its greatest asset. Her employer took a different approach to alleviating the pinch of a bad economy: "We have asked all of our team members for cost-saving suggestions and ideas on how we can get through these tough times without a layoff. To date, we have saved a tremendous amount of money and haven't displaced a single worker ... I am proud to be associated with a company that Walks the Talk."

When leadership conducts layoffs with integrity—making an effort to avoid them, honestly explaining and demonstrating why they are needed, and carrying them out with fairness and compassion—they at least partially alleviate the anger and anxiety associated with such actions.

Walking the Talk

Actions speak louder than words, especially the actions of leaders. Four-Star General Wilbur "Bill" Creech understood that quite well when he took charge of the U.S. Air Force's Tactical Air Command (TAC) in 1978. At the time, TAC was failing in its mission of training pilots to survive combat. TAC's strategies were outmoded, its facilities and equipment deteriorating, its morale at a dangerously low altitude.

In a "Dear Boss" letter, published in a military journal a few months after General Creech's appointment, an Air Force captain assigned to TAC announced his resignation and summarized his reasons: "Long hours with little support, entitlements eroded, integrity a mockery, zero visible career progression and senior commanders evidently totally missing the point."

FOCUS

"Integrity is simply a yes-or-no question. You either have it or you don't. For that reason, leaders must always display the highest standards of integrity."

—General Ronald R. Fogleman, Chief of Staff (Retired), United States Air Force

General Creech acknowledged that TAC had lost its way. "The thrust was on saving money ... It overlooked the requirement to do a good job," he told an interviewer years later.

He made it his mission to transform TAC into an organization of combat-ready flight crews, trained under realistic battle conditions and supported by small, closely knit teams ready to operate a minute after arriving in a war zone. His arsenal included both grand tactics and small gestures.

General Creech once swapped a supply sergeant's decrepit chair—it was patched with duct tape and propped on a brick—with the quite nice desk chair belonging to the general in charge of logistics. Creech told the general that he could have his chair back after he improved his supply pipeline. General Creech believed that leaders shouldn't expect quality work from workers who are shabbily treated.

A Wink, a Nod, and a Salute

As he did with the decrepit chair, General Creech sometimes drove a point home in a roundabout way. When he noticed a soldier who didn't salute officers, he would invite that soldier back to his office, make conversation, and eventually call the man's squadron commander to retrieve him.

"All I'd say to the commander was, 'He seems like an awfully fine young person, but apparently he hasn't been to school for military discipline, so I'm sure you're going to take time to do that because I wouldn't like to see you up here too often.'"

Creech's subtle but firm techniques enlisted subordinate officers in enforcing discipline. At the same time, he put the officers on notice to do their jobs more effectively. He achieved his objectives without having to issue a general notice regarding the need to salute superior officers.

Fair Is Fair

General Creech summarized his values in a list of four pass/fail conditions that would result in immediate dismissal:

- Any kind of integrity violation
- Ruling through fear or terror
- Losing one's temper in public
- Any kind of abuse of office

Upholding these values was more important, even, than passing an operational readiness inspection. Creech held both low-level and high-level offenders to the same standards, and he wasted no time in handing out punishments for violations.

The general permanently grounded an F-15 pilot who nearly ran out of fuel while making an unauthorized detour over his hometown in Texas and then lied when questioned about the flight. A similar fate befell the brigadier general who ordered his squadron to perform an unscheduled flyby over an air base in Germany after completing a rigorous 12-hour deployment flight. In the confusion of the flyby, two airmen mistakenly ejected. Like the Texas pilot, the brigadier general tried to cover up his breach of flight discipline. Creech offered him two choices: retire or be court-martialed.

Although the brigadier general initially grounded the two pilots who ejected, Creech later reinstated them. He recognized the difference between their mistake and their superior officer's deliberate failure of integrity. An effective leader recognizes when people make honest mistakes.

Measurable Results Mount

The general reshaped the Air Force's training methods and combat tactics and supervised the design, selection, and purchase of modern military aircraft. Under his six-year command, TAC's accident rate declined from 7.6 to 2 per 100,000 hours, flight sorties each month doubled, and the number of aircraft grounded for maintenance diminished by 75 percent. His policies increased TAC productivity by 80 percent and saved the U.S. government $12 billion. His officer-training program produced 21 four-star generals, including a future Chairman of the Joint Chiefs of Staff.

General Creech had values, vision, and a mission—and he walked the talk.

Developing Relationships

When you build a relationship of mutual loyalty and respect with your employees, they're more willing to go the extra mile on the company's behalf. Loyal employees who feel valued by their company show an increased commitment to producing quality products and services.

Effective leaders recognize the value of relationships. Some go to almost extraordinary lengths to create them. That's what the executive team of the Harley-Davidson Motorcycle Company did in the mid-1990s. The company implemented a "close-to-the-customer" philosophy, pledging to put customer satisfaction above all else. Nothing unusual about that. But Harley-Davidson took the concept much further, creating a partnership with its unions to carry out the customer-first pledge. Management and union leaders became allies on the customers' behalf.

The company lived up to its values by including union representatives in every aspect of decision-making. At a time when the strength of unions nationally had deteriorated to new lows, Harley-Davidson's executive team even consulted its unions on the location of a new plant—when it would have been easy to undercut their influence by building in a right-to-work state.

Union leaders reciprocated. When quality problems developed on a production line and the plant's managers were out of town, the unions could have shut down the line and gone home. But they didn't. A union officer identified the cause and got the problem fixed, and production resumed within an hour. By going beyond the bounds of duty, union and management exemplified the stated value of putting customer satisfaction first.

If you suspect Harley-Davidson's bottom line was affected by the collaboration with unions, you're right. Its long-term earnings grew an average of 37 percent a year, and its equity value increased by 400 percent in a 15-year period.

Admitting Mistakes

Admitting mistakes is a sign of strength, not weakness. In surveys of more than 38,000 people, the Institute for Health and Human Potential found that willingness to freely admit making a mistake is "the single most important variable in contributing to the career advancement of a leader." People who admit to screwing up are more likely to learn from their mistakes and are more likely to be risk-takers. Leaders who admit mistakes are more likely to encourage an atmosphere of learning and growth.

Confucius, the Chinese philosopher who preached the value of personal morality and justice, once said, "A man who has committed a mistake and doesn't correct it is committing another mistake."

After the failed Bay of Pigs invasion, President John F. Kennedy paraphrased Confucius. Accepting personal responsibility for the fiasco, President Kennedy told newspaper publishers, "This

Administration intends to be candid about its errors; for as a wise man once said, 'An error does not become a mistake until you refuse to correct it.' We intend to accept full responsibility for our errors and we expect you to point them out when we miss them."

The Bay of Pigs was one of the country's biggest foreign policy failures, but Kennedy turned the invasion into a leadership lesson by admitting his mistake and taking steps to avoid the same missteps in the future. He was almost embarrassed by the fact that his approval ratings soared after the admission. Additionally, after the invasion, President Kennedy encouraged more debate and disagreement among his advisors. Like President Kennedy, you should strive to learn from your mistakes. But you can't learn from them unless you acknowledge them. Admission is also the fastest path to putting the mistakes behind you—and in this era of Twitter and YouTube, it's crazy to believe a mistake can remain hidden for long.

By nature, humans don't like to admit mistakes. We're wired to rationalize our decisions, to look for evidence that supports our actions. Some experts say this urge is so strong that we can convince ourselves that we're right even when everyone around us can see that we're wrong. If your audience of "everyone else" is your workforce, you're putting your credibility at risk.

"When a leader makes a mistake and doesn't admit it, he is seen as arrogant and untrustworthy," says Duke University Basketball Coach Mike Krzyzewski, an expert in leadership development. "And 'untrustworthy,' is the last thing a leader wants to be."

Leadership Lessons Served with Popcorn

Numerous academic studies have researched leadership styles and their effectiveness, but John Ford's 1955 film *Mister Roberts* beats them all with an illustration of leadership principles. The film, often screened in leadership training classes, is based on the now widely accepted theory that recognition as a leader can only be earned from those willing to follow.

Henry Fonda is Mister Roberts, the cargo officer on the USS *Reluctant*, a World War II supply ship operating far out of the line of fire. Roberts is desperate to fight in the "real" war, on a real battleship. James Cagney is the ship's despotic Captain Morton, willing to use coercive tactics to achieve results that make him look good.

The captain and Mister Roberts occupy opposite ends of the leadership spectrum. Captain Morton, nominal leader of the ship, represents a command-and-control leadership style. He couldn't care less about his team's needs and desires. Mister Roberts embodies a collaborative leadership style. He knows and cares about each person, inspiring his crew to higher levels of achievement and loyalty.

Still, Mister Roberts wants off the ship, which "sails from Tedium to Apathy and back again, with an occasional side trip to Monotony," so that he can contribute to the war effort. In his mind, transporting dungarees, toothpaste, and toilet paper isn't really contributing. But when he gets his transfer, Mister Roberts realizes the *Reluctant*'s crew is playing an important part in the war.

"The unseen enemy of this war," he writes to his former shipmates, "is the boredom that eventually becomes a faith and, therefore, a terrible sort of suicide" for those who don't know their part in achieving a greater goal. The letter expresses what is now leadership gospel: people want to be part of a cause bigger than themselves.

These themes—collaborative leadership, meaningful work, and the relationships between leaders and their followers—are explored throughout the rest of this book.

Leader, Know Thyself!

In This Chapter

- Looking into the four primary personality types
- Considering the pros and cons of each type
- Communicating with different personalities

Categorizing leadership styles is like looking for the ultimate bread recipe—thousands of variations exist, but every loaf of bread is essentially a combination of flour, water, and salt. Identifying styles of leadership is the same: every year, authors publish half a dozen new books on the topic, but in the end, they all end up talking about four primary personality types.

As with bread, your individual leadership style depends on the proportion of "ingredients," what "seasonings" you add, and the environment in which you "bake" it. And just like bread, the many variations are what make leadership style such an endlessly fascinating topic.

The advice "know thyself"—so basic, it's like the flour in bread—was inscribed on the Temple of Apollo, home of the first self-help goddess, the Oracle of Delphi. Humanity has been exploring the theme ever since. But the ancient Greeks nailed it. The route to determining your leadership style—to knowing who you are— is self-reflection. Additionally, the ability to recognize behavior patterns in others gives you insight into how they may react in certain situations. Such insight enables you to modify your behavior to interact more effectively.

Getting a Grip on Personality Types

Your personality—the way you behave, think, and feel—comes from within. It's a shimmery thing, like the reflection on a lake. You can't put your finger on it or define it completely. Thankfully, social scientists have found ways to evaluate and catalog the emotions, values, and feelings associated with our personalities.

Harvard psychologist William Mouton Marston introduced the idea of typing behavior into four categories in 1928. Researchers have expanded and refined Marston's method, but most personality surveys are still based on the same four areas of behavior developed by Marston:

- Response to problems and challenges
- Ability to influence others
- Preferred pace of environment
- Compliance with procedures and rules

The answers you give on behavioral surveys help psychologists determine whether you're task-oriented or people-focused, an extrovert or an introvert. Other traits exist within those broad categories, including patterns of communication, risk-taking, comfort with conflict, and ability to deal with change. The one or two characteristics that predominate—whether in unusually high or low proportions—define your type. (Most of us call this personality testing, but I've been assured—warned, even—that "personality test" is a very loose term.)

FOCUS

Everyone exhibits behavior from all four personality types, just to different degrees. The combinations of characteristics—those varying "recipes"—make us unique.

The four broad categories of behavior types are as follows:

- Restless Driver
- Social Influencer
- Steady Eddie
- Compliant Analytic

I describe each of the four personality types in detail in the following sections.

Knowing your style—better yet, yours and that of all your co-workers—enables you to understand the behavioral language they're speaking. Just think how much better we would all get along if we could all make adjustments and learn a few words of the other guy's language.

Note: I pulled my overview of the four primary personality styles from the many assessment systems available. To avoid mimicking any one brand, I gave each style a new label, which reflects its identifying characteristics.

 FOCUS

Knowing your boss's behavioral style is as important as knowing your own and your co-workers' styles, a point made in the U.S. Army's *Handbook on Small Unit Leadership:*

"Unit leaders must assess how the boss communicates and how information is received. Some use direct and personal contact while others may be more comfortable with weekly meetings, electronic mail, or memoranda. Knowing the boss's intent, priorities, and thought processes enhance organizational effectiveness and success."

Restless Drivers: Task-Oriented Extroverts

Restless Drivers are, well, restless and driven. They're direct, strong-willed, assertive, and decisive. Drivers are often entrepreneurs who are hell-bent on success, even if they seem to be doing everything by the seat of their pants. When there's a fire, call a Driver.

Drivers forge ahead. They're quick thinkers and quick to act. They like being in charge. Drivers believe in themselves and their version of the facts. Drivers come across as self-confident, which leads those around them to view them as competent. (By the way, just because someone is self-confident doesn't always mean that they are competent.) They are ambitious, determined, and competitive. They're also curious and adventurous.

On the dark side: Restless Drivers do have a few blind spots. They tend to believe that everyone else thinks and reacts the way they do. They move so quickly that they don't notice the wake of blank, uncomprehending looks behind them. What they consider to be self-confidence, others may call abrasive. Drivers are surprised when they hear themselves described as bullies or autocrats.

Pet peeves: People who ramble on with tedious details (never mind that everyone else considers them necessary details); being stuck—at a desk, in a job, or in a pool of boredom for more than five minutes; and not being in charge, so that things would move faster.

Restless Drivers need to learn: To be quiet and listen, even if the other speaker occasionally rambles; to manage their impatience; and to take time to make informed decisions—and give others the chance to do the same. Drivers should wake up to the perception that they are arrogant and rude, even though that's not what they intend.

> **BREAK POINT**
>
> Nothing could be more painful for a Restless Driver than listening to a Steady Eddie—make that slow-and-Steady Eddie—plow through a mountain of "pointless" details. The Driver would chew glass to avoid such conversations—even when Steady Eddie is pointing out that the business is failing.

Social Influencers: People-Focused Extroverts

Social Influencers are enthusiastic, charismatic, trusting, and optimistic. They see a sunny future and use their passion to get others to see it, too. They're often called visionary and charismatic. They spin stories that inspire and energize others.

Influencers multitask, enjoy fast-paced environments, and draw energy from new people, projects, and especially public recognition. In the eyes of the Influencer, everyone has potential, a mission in life, and a way to achieve it. They're team-oriented but don't necessarily want to lead because they view leading as involving too much work.

On the dark side: Social Influencers are visionary but have a distaste for details. They wilt when held to a schedule or required to perform mundane tasks. Looking to the future can mean overlooking what needs to be done here and now. Unfinished projects fall by the wayside. At their worst, Influencers come across as shameless self-promoters. Under stress, they come unglued.

Pet peeves: Being forced into a schedule created by others; the monotony of routine—any routine; paperwork; and being ignored or chastised.

Social Influencers need to learn: To curb their enthusiasm long enough to complete the current project; to develop self-discipline and time-management skills; and to be more discriminating when trusting others.

BREAK POINT

Nothing brings down the gregarious Social Influencer like pessimistic, task-oriented, noncommunicative introverts—in other words, a Compliant Analytic.

Steady Eddies: People-Focused Introverts

Steady Eddies are like turtles: deliberate, steady, stable, and amiable. Eddies listen and are patient, dependable, supportive, and loyal. They get satisfaction from working in a close-knit team, and they strive for workplace harmony, sometimes to the point of turning away from trouble.

Eddies are devoted to the organization and its people. They want to know what's expected and be appreciated—without fanfare—when they deliver. As leaders, they're more flexible and supportive than people with more task-oriented styles. Eddies' decisions are based on instinct and emotion. Poker-faced and quiet, Eddies don't lead with drama or flair, rather by building relationships. When problems arise, their go-to solution is avoidance.

On the dark side: Change, especially sudden change, is the biggest challenge for Steady Eddies. They don't deal well with aggressive or confrontational people and will cave to avoid conflict. Eddies are nondemonstrative, giving the impression of not caring. Like a turtle, when pushed, Eddie slows down and withdraws.

Pet peeves: Lack of appreciation for hard work; people who grab credit for someone else's results; and feeling unfairly criticized or unsupported.

Steady Eddies need to learn: To loosen up a little—too much routine turns them into the Tin Man; to let others know what they're thinking or feeling; and to learn to accept and, if not embrace change, at least give it a tentative hug.

BREAK POINT

Steady Eddies are unnerved by the ever-shifting energy and attention of Restless Drivers. Before an Eddie gets enough momentum to say what needs to be said, the Driver has moved on, often literally out the door. Changes that the Driver finds invigorating only increase the Eddie's anxiety.

Compliant Analytics: Task-Focused Introverts

Compliant Analytics are cautious, careful, quiet, and, above all, they want to avoid making a mistake. They live in fear of a flaw—a flaw, not a failure. They're data-heads and are exacting and systematic. They plan for and anticipate problems before they occur. Your project is in good hands with an Analytic.

Analytics dress carefully, tend to behave rather formally, and are all business all the time. They may be nearly silent, but they are observant. They would live in the nitty-gritty details if they could, which makes them quite certain of their facts. Don't be surprised if an Analytic quotes television detective Adrian Monk: "I could be wrong … But I don't think so."

Because they are so detail-oriented, Analytics can be effective leaders, so long as they recognize and fight their compulsion to micromanage.

On the dark side: Compliant Analytics like to thoroughly evaluate the consequences of any potential action—so much so, they suffer analysis paralysis. When times get tough, an Analytic finds security in standards and process. They are loathe to share thoughts or opinions.

Pet peeves: Questions from people who—as far as the Analytic is concerned—don't understand what's happening; working in an environment where quality control is lax; and watching extroverted colleagues get credit for the quality of his work because he doesn't speak up and claim it.

Compliant Analytics need to learn: That sometimes good enough is good enough; to stop worrying so much about being wrong; and how to speak up for themselves.

BREAK POINT

Social Influencers are as different from Compliant Analytics as you can get. Influencers are social, not aloof; they're impulsive in the eyes of the disapproving Analytic; they think big thoughts about the future, but won't do what it takes to get there.

Bridging the Gaps Between Personality Types

People receive information more readily when it's delivered in their preferred style. For example, a woman complains to her girlfriend that her husband never says "I love you." "But he brings you flowers every Tuesday," the girlfriend replies. "That's saying 'I love you,' isn't it?" "Yes," says the wife, "But that's not how I want to hear it."

Most of us forget that people take in information better when it's delivered in their preferred style. Unless we only talk to people like ourselves, our messages will keep falling through the cracks. It's up to the person delivering the message to use the recipient's communication style.

BREAK POINT

So often, one person says something to another and believes communication has taken place. Wrong! Information has to be received and understood, not just conveyed, to count as communication.

Deciphering Messages

Bill, a Restless Driver who owns a popular restaurant, talks over his shoulder as he walks toward his building's back door. A slender man in a suit and tie—in contrast to Bill's Hawaiian shirt—follows tentatively, trying to hand Bill a folder.

"Yeah, Dave, yeah. Listen, I don't have time right now to sit down and talk, but let's do it next week, okay?" He's seen the folder in Dave's hands and just knows he wants to go over a dreary list of receivables. Bill has been dancing away from Dave, a Steady Eddie, for about six weeks. Dave, usually content to retreat to his office, seems oddly determined to talk today.

Bill twirls his keychain, trying to signal an urgent appointment somewhere—anywhere. Dave is uncharacteristically persistent.

"Bill," he says, "You can go. But I just want to let you know— you've got just about enough cash for two weeks. Then we shut the doors."

Dave stops talking, anxiety creasing his forehead. He isn't kidding. He's seen the problem coming, but every time he tries to bring it up, Bill ducks out. Dave feels awful for letting things get out of hand, but Bill can be so barky. Dave hates that.

"Just give me the bottom line," Bill says, pushing Dave's folder away. "Two weeks? Why didn't you speak up sooner? I gotta go take care of this."

This is a classic case of missed messages and miscommunication between two men who see each other four or five days a week. They've been working together three years, but they still don't communicate—not even when they talk. Neither Dave nor Bill has any clue how the other wants to "hear" a message.

FOCUS

"The single biggest problem in communication is the illusion that it has taken place."

—George Bernard Shaw, playwright

Dave and Bill are opposites when it comes to conveying information, especially when the subject is negative. Dave's been dreading this talk; he's been happy to let Bill slide out of it up until now. He just wishes Bill would let him explain what's been going on. But he can hardly get a sentence out before Bill jumps ahead and ask questions.

Bill can't stand looking at numbers. He doesn't even like to see more than one sheet of paper. Dave drones on forever and Bill can't help it—he gets antsy. Dave's communication mantra is "Don't bore me with the details!"

If Dave thought about it, he could have put the problem in bullet points on a single sheet, delivered it to Bill, and said, "Let me know if you have questions."

Just the thought of talking to Bill, though, churns Dave's stomach. You'd never know it by looking at him, but he's afraid of Dave's temper. The week before, Bill burst into Dave's office to ask him to deliver a vendor's check. He barked out the directions so fast, Dave didn't have time to pick up a pencil. Luckily the address was on the check.

Communicating with Different Personalities

I'm going to tell you how to communicate with each of the four primary personality styles. Because I'm like Bill and tend to be a Restless Driver, I've put it in a bulleted list:

- **Restless Driver:** One coaching organization puts it this way: "Be bright, be brief, be gone." Get right to the point, then follow up with written documentation or background information. Don't launch into descriptive stories. Be ready with quick answers; you won't have time to ponder your response.

- **Social Influencer:** No red flags here, Influencers are masters of the communications universe. Leave time for chit-chat; keep the business conversation general, with details to follow. Put on your happy face.

- **Steady Eddie:** Eddies need time to prepare, so provide an early agenda, if possible; don't spring any last-minute surprise topics; be friendly, warm, and appreciative of their effort; don't be sarcastic or say anything flippant, as their feelings are easily bruised.

- **Compliant Analytic:** Analytics prefer written communication, the less person-to-person the better; don't deliver anything that's not perfect, or you'll never hear the end of it; give them time to think, and don't interrupt. Don't be casual, pushy, or boisterous in any way. Don't ask about their personal lives—and don't share yours.

Remember that it's up to you to make sure the recipient understands your message. That means modifying your style to theirs. Compare your communication strategy to releasing a movie. If you're producing videotapes but your audience prefers online streaming, chances are you aren't going to reach them.

Putting Communication Strategies to Work

Nobody enjoys reprimanding or firing a subordinate. Yet, if you're in a management position for very long, you're going to have to deal with underperforming employees. Although reprimanding or even terminating an employee is never a pleasant experience, you can turn it into a more positive experience by paying attention to your individual communication style and harnessing it to your advantage.

The following sections include examples of the four personality styles and how people who have those styles might deal with Joe, a senior employee in a key position, who hasn't been performing up to standards for many months. He has just committed another mistake, blowing a $250,000 contract. How might leaders from the four primary styles handle this situation? Would it make a difference whether they know their individual styles and recognize their weaknesses?

Restless Driver: Take Early Action

The Restless Driver is first up. He blows his stack. He's been watching the pile-up coming but said nothing. This last disaster sends him over the edge.

He strides into Joe's office with blood vessels bulging and berates him, not bothering to close the door. He reminds Joe of the "many, many times I warned you that things were going south," then summarily tells Joe he's "terminated immediately." Joe is left struggling to recall any conversation in which the boss warned of coming trouble.

If the Driver was aware of his tendency toward angry outbursts, he might have managed his temper at least enough to fire Joe in a less abusive way. Instead, he allowed himself to rant and then acted on an impulsive decision.

He could have made his directness work to his advantage, instead of against him, by bluntly discussing Joe's disappointing performance when the problem started. If he'd checked to make sure Joe had the resources to do his job right—he still didn't know— and offered some one-on-one support, this latest screw-up might have been avoided. And if Joe hadn't improved after that, at least the Driver could better justify terminating Joe.

He might not have made such a hasty decision if he'd left the building when he felt the thunderclouds of anger gathering in his head. He could have vented, then talked to Joe. The Driver should adopt the idea of "sleeping on" any decision made while he is angry or impatient (this won't be easy, because Drivers accomplish a lot when they're angry or impatient). Great leaders manage their emotions and maintain composure.

Social Influencer: Curb Your Compassion

The Social Influencer really, really doesn't want to deal with this situation. She is painfully aware Joe's wife has been sick. And it's nearly Christmas, after all. She knows so much about Joe's family that they're practically friends.

She's seen him failing. She didn't talk to him about it, but she praised every little accomplishment, hoping to inspire improvement. Her efforts didn't work. Every time she started the dreaded performance review, she ended up dishing about office politics. The situation is just so uncomfortable.

Knowing her own style won't make this Influencer any more comfortable with sitting Joe down and issuing a warning. But as Dr. Phil says, you can't solve a problem until you face it. Joe isn't a friend; he's a longtime employee who is failing but deserves a shot at redemption. If the Influencer is really a leader, she has to put aside her squeamishness.

Joe is something of a Restless Driver, with the Driver's short attention span, high self-confidence, resistance to authority, and low tolerance for long discussions. This is a problem for the Influencer, who rambles, socializes, and veers off topic. So if the Influencer wants to get her message across to Joe, she must be clear and remain focused. She needs to deliver it in his style, not hers, to make sure it sinks in.

Reluctantly but resolutely, she plans a 15-minute conversation (in her mind, that's potential for high conflict). "We're going to have to keep this short, Joe," she says. "I do have to tell you we're not happy with your performance." She's not surprised when he interrupts; he always does. But she's ready. She cuts him off. "I want you to be successful, but I do have to explain what is wrong. Here are four incidents from the last four months."

Familiar with Joe's style as well as her own, the Influencer sucked up her courage and did what had to be done, in the way it had to be done. In the future, she should be understanding but less lenient. When she finds herself regularly justifying the poor performance of others, the Influencer should reassert the requirements of a job well done and make sure there are consequences for less-than-optimal effort.

Steady Eddie: Face Up to Conflict

Steady Eddie has been picking up the slack for Joe. No one knows except his wife, who listens to him moan about it every night. Steady doesn't want to shatter office harmony by confronting or firing Joe. He's maintaining his poker face—everyone else thinks he either doesn't notice or doesn't care about the problem. Office morale is sinking.

Like the Social Influencer, Steady Eddie fears conflict with a Restless Driver like Joe. So Eddie prepares himself for the discussion by writing a one-page memo with the four points he needs to convey to Joe. He also writes a follow-up memo, explaining each point at length—this is more for his benefit than Joe's, because Eddie needs to feel completely prepared. He sends Joe an email, setting up an appointment to talk in a quiet place; he tells Joe to schedule at least 30 minutes.

Steady Eddie has to recognize his own style as well as Joe's. For himself, he must be thoroughly prepared; for Joe, he must find a way to deliver his message succinctly and directly. The one-page memo keeps him moving in the conversation, while the follow-up memo satisfies his need to be thorough.

Steady Eddie has to realize that the appearance of harmony can be deceiving. He needs to force himself to have more uncomfortable conversations—he's not doing anyone any favors by being unwilling to call someone to task for not doing a good job.

If he had thought about it as soon as Joe's performance began to falter, Eddie might have restrained himself from picking up the slack. Instead, he could have sent Joe an email, noting each shortcoming and spelling out the consequences if the situation didn't improve. Joe would have been on notice, and Eddie wouldn't have suffered the frustration of doing someone else's work.

Firing a subordinate is one of the most difficult leadership tasks, one rarely done well, especially by a Steady. Relationships are sacred to him.

Compliant Analytic: Call for Backup

The Compliant Analytic is going berserk—quietly. The only time he really speaks up is if someone challenges his facts. He's been sitting at Joe's desk for six weeks in an all-out micromanaging assault. The longer he's there, the less Joe does. It's not just that Joe is failing; the Analytic sees his own inability to fix the situation as his failure. He keeps trying "one last thing."

Ironically, it's one of the Analytic's "curses"—his extreme attention to detail—that made it easiest for him, among the leadership styles, to recognize Joe's problem early. The Restless Driver and the Social Influencer weren't paying close attention. Steady Eddie hoped the problem would evaporate before he opened his eyes.

An extreme Analytic is the least likely to be able to "fix" Joe, fire him, or step away from the problem and admit defeat. He will continue to sit at Joe's side. It remains to be seen who will break first—the Analytic, from his anxiety, or Joe, who's ready to strangle his micromanaging boss.

Ideally, the Analytic can call a human resources executive to deal with the Joe problem. Left to his own devices, he should follow the lead of Steady Eddie and prepare a written list of talking points. The reason he has more trouble than the other three types is that the Analytic is driven by the fear of failure—and, in this case, he failed to fix Joe when the problem first developed.

He doesn't have any problems imposing high standards—he is just extremely reluctant to confront the person who isn't achieving those standards. Like the Social Influencer and Steady Eddie, the Compliant Analytic needs training in how to have more uncomfortable conversations.

Under stress, we default to doing what we've always done—generally the worst possible option. The Restless Driver exploded; the Social Influencer dithered as long as she could; Steady Eddie kept his back turned and his head down; while the detail-oriented, perfectionist Compliant Analytic couldn't resist his urge to tinker with the problem—he should have seen it coming! It's not always possible, but leaders of every behavioral type benefit from having deputies with complementary styles—I think of them as supporting cast members—to handle tasks for which the leader isn't particularly well-suited.

Which Style Is Best?

No style or combination of styles is best. Early management theorists tried developing a "one-size-fits-all" leader model ideal for every situation. That theory was replaced by its opposite; a leader should be hired for specific situations and environments. That idea spun through the revolving door along with the realization that organizations couldn't hire fast enough to keep up with change.

A more relevant question is this: which combination of styles makes the best leadership team? Some styles mesh like a patch on a screen door; others might as well have been created on different planets.

The current tweak in management theory is that leaders should slide from one style to another as events unfold. Many leaders do that out of necessity. But you can only change so much, softening some behaviors and boosting others. People who try to put on a full "style disguise" come across as inauthentic, get less done, and are unhappier at work.

Why not just cozy up to your inner self and examine your behavior patterns? Contemplate the reasons for your successes and your failures. If you know where you're likely to trip up, you can modify your behavior and avoid those pitfalls.

FOCUS

Self-knowledge is important for leaders. Just ask Google: I typed the statement "self-knowledge is important for leaders" into the internet search engine, and within 0.19 seconds was rewarded with 12.6 million results.

Communication: More Than Just Talk

In This Chapter

- Planning your communication strategy
- Being aware of your audience
- Identifying the key communicators in your organization
- Listening to and accepting criticism

"Because I say so!" is no longer an acceptable response when someone questions a leadership directive or voices a contrary opinion. As a leader, you want to generate consent rather than demand it.

To generate consent, you need strong communication skills. The best communicators use a conversational, not coercive, tone, and what they say reflects their values. If your message isn't sincere, people are likely to ignore you or misunderstand you. And if, by chance, you think that silence will suffice, you're wrong. The less you say as a leader, the more others will say about you.

Leaders are responsible for both internal and external communication. Internally, leaders talk to their employees or team members. Externally, they reach out to stockholders, business partners, customers, and the community—anyone with a vested interest in the message. I touch on communicating with external stakeholders in this chapter, but my focus is on communicating within your organization.

Developing a Communication Strategy

To be an effective leader you need to develop a solid communication strategy. A communication strategy is a core message that reflects an organization's overall agenda, values, purpose, and mission. You can use your strategy as a tool to coordinate messages to all stakeholders—internal and external—to influence policy or public opinion, promote a brand, enhance reputation, or motivate participation. A communication strategy has both short-term and long-term goals.

Communication of any kind—advertising, news reports, fiction—is a form of storytelling. Although some storytelling is purely for entertainment, organizational communication must convey a clear message. You want to persuade recipients of the message's validity and, in the case of team members, solidify their commitment to your mission and influence their actions in achieving your common goals.

When developing your communication strategy—your story— carefully consider the message, compose it thoughtfully, and then be consistent about conveying it. Use the resulting strategy to inform every action you take and every message you send. An effective communication strategy dovetails with your organizational agenda.

Integrate your communication strategy with your mission and your overall business strategy. Although communication in this day and age is no longer exclusively a matter of top-down pronouncements, your story and your strategy must start at the top of the organization. If the boss doesn't buy into it—and live by it—neither will anyone else.

Strategic Communication Is an Effective Tool

Businesses and organizations ranging in size from one-person operations to worldwide organizations have communication strategies. No less than the U.S. Joint Forces Command has a handbook outlining a communication strategy for fighting the war in Afghanistan. The handbook details in 232 pages— including Appendixes A through Q and 42 illustrations—the "Battle of the Narrative," which is "not merely to push aside, defeat or gain superiority over the enemy's narrative—it is to completely supplant it."

If you doubt how seriously the U.S. military views the importance of communication as a weapon in the war, here's Admiral James Stavridis, of the U.S. Southern Command of the Joint Forces in Afghanistan, talking about his mission in the war: "At Southern Command, Strategic Communication is our main battery. We're in the business of launching ideas, not Tomahawk missiles."

Communication strategy is every bit as vital as physical battle, according to the *Commanders Handbook*, which notes somewhat ruefully that the United States was slow to come to this realization: "Victory in the long war ultimately depends on strategic communication by the United States and its international partners. Effective communication must build and maintain credibility and trust with friends and foes alike ... Such credibility is essential to building trusted networks that counter ideological support for terrorism."

The enemy, on the other hand, recognized that front of the war early on, as outlined in a message from one Al Qaeda leader to another: "... I say to you: that we are in a battle and that more than half of this battle is taking place in the battlefield of the media. And that we are in a media battle in a race for the hearts and minds of our Umma." The word *race* isn't used lightly; the United States has timed how long it takes Al Qaeda to respond publicly to any significant U.S. initiative: 26 minutes.

Nine Principles of Strategic Communication

Whether your communication strategy is a simple document or, like the *Commanders Handbook*, lengthy and littered with acronyms, the basic principles are the same. Any effective communication strategy must have the following characteristics:

- **Leadership-driven:** Embrace and enact at the executive level
- **Credible:** Base the strategy on truthfulness and respect
- **Dialogue:** Allow an exchange of multifaceted ideas
- **Unity:** Integrate and coordinate the message at all levels
- **Responsive:** Right message, right time, right audience
- **Understanding:** Focus on recipients' interests
- **Pervasive:** Every action or inaction sends a message
- **Results-based:** Use metrics to assess effectiveness
- **Continuous:** Analyze, plan, execute, assess, and then repeat

I adapted this list from the Principles of Strategic Communication Guide, signed and published by the U.S. Department of Defense in 2008. You can find similar principles—under other names or packaged differently—in dozens of academic or commercial publications on communications.

Cultural Awareness

Just because you're talking doesn't mean you're communicating. If the target of your message doesn't "get" it, you haven't communicated. The person trying to get a message across is responsible for communicating that message in a form the recipient understands.

In Chapter 2, I stressed the importance of understanding the other person's style in any one-to-one conversation. When you're communicating to your entire organization or one of its departments, or to an outside community group, you want to understand the culture of the group. This is particularly true since communication is often a means of implementing major organizational changes, and culture plays a big part in how change is viewed and accepted.

Know Your Audience

If you're president of a community college, the culture and communication style of your Faculty Senate is different from that of the maintenance and security personnel, the support staff's union, the Board of Trustees, and the students. If you work for an IT company, your sales force and your engineering teams probably need to get your message in different formats or language.

FOCUS

Research by the Studer Group, encompassing more than 2,000 health-care leaders, indicates that when you use the word *mandatory* to describe a new process, 98 percent of employees understand they must comply. If you use the word *required,* only 68 percent realize they must follow the process. If you say that compliance *is expected,* only 26 percent recognize they have no choice but to comply.

The lesson from this study? State your expectations clearly and directly.

As a leader, you tailor the way you deliver your message to each of your constituencies. (Notice I'm not saying you deliver different messages—that's the kiss of death if you want to maintain credibility.)

Likewise, be sure to address the interests and concerns of your employees, not just your own. As CEO, you may be most concerned about increasing recognition of your brand; however, your employees may be worrying about the increasing cost of parking in your business district. As commander of a U.S. Army unit in a war zone, you're concerned about seemingly unprovoked attacks on soldiers visiting a village; villagers may still be smoldering over the destruction of the local school by international forces two years earlier. Only by addressing the concerns of all factions can you ensure that the message that most concerns you, as a leader, is warmly received.

Buy-In Begins at the Beginning

The most effective way to get employees to buy into your organizational goals is to invite their participation in developing those goals. That means inviting input from the start of the process. The best organizational messages meld the objectives and interests of leadership and employees. By inviting, even insisting on, contributions from the rank and file from the start, your organization's narrative will elicit more commitment at every level.

Including team members or employees at the earliest stages may seem cumbersome and more time-consuming than announcing your intentions at a company meeting. And it's true, you want to keep the process structured and focused. But front-loading participation has two obvious advantages that make it worthwhile. First, people will accept the end product—your mission, goals, and strategy—more readily because they had a hand in its creation. Second, you'll have access to a wider range of ideas and viewpoints than if you relied only on your "usual suspects" to create policy and strategy.

That's the tack taken by the leadership team at Infosys, when that IT consulting company invited people from all divisions to describe significant trends affecting customers. The result was a list of 17 trends, which then became topics of online forums. After compiling the list, company leaders again asked employees for this input by suggesting service solutions the company could offer customers in response to the trends.

Letting people contribute to the design of their own projects, in the way Infosys did, is one way of keeping them involved in and satisfied with their work. For more information on the benefits of keeping employees engaged, turn to Chapter 6.

Who Carries Out Your Communication Strategy?

Everyone in your organization has a role to play in carrying out your communication strategy. The following sections outline the key players and how you can get them involved.

The Executive Team

As part of the executive team, you have primary responsibility for shaping the strategy and leading the communications charge. You set the standard for sharing information, listening carefully, and responding to feedback.

> **FOCUS**
>
> "The leader must be able to share knowledge and ideas to transmit a sense of urgency and enthusiasm to others. If a leader can't get a message across clearly and motivate others to act on it, then having a message doesn't even matter."
>
> —Gilbert Amelio, President and CEO, National Semiconductor Corp.

Supervisors

Don't be afraid to empower supervisors to be key communicators. These employees include military officers of all ranks, shop stewards and foremen, project team leaders, heads of sales, and lead technicians on the help desks. Innumerable studies show that people want important information to come from their supervisors. Enabling these people to speak for you builds their credibility.

The Rank-and-File

No longer relegated to being seen and not heard, rank-and-file employees are a key component in your communication strategy. These people often have their ears to the ground and the most interaction with your customers. As a result, they take on a variety of roles—insightful observers, brand ambassadors, Greek chorus, sometime critics, out-of-the-box innovators, pulse-takers, and sounding boards.

Leaders Communicate Authenticity, Clarity, and Direction

As a leader, you want to harness your communication to build bonds of trust and loyalty that not only benefit you, but everyone else involved. As in any relationship, trust and loyalty grow gradually. Someone has to take the first steps, and as the leader, you should be the one taking those first steps.

Authentic communication involves personal revelation. That doesn't mean you're going to share your personal problems with everyone in your organization. It does mean that you allow others to see your personal response to a situation. For example, when Facebook's stock price fell by half shortly after the company went public, it was weeks before Mark Zuckerberg, the company founder, made any public comment on the topic. When Zuckerberg finally did admit his disappointment, the stock rallied—it was as though people were waiting for an indication that Zuckerberg cared.

Authentic communication implies some degree of vulnerability—an idea that makes some leaders uncomfortable. When you're willing to make yourself vulnerable in some aspects of communication—for example, how you developed your value system—you'll reap the benefits in the form of trust in other areas—for example, when you announce bad news that will require sacrifice from everyone.

And although your overall communication strategy probably includes branding, mass communications to both internal and external audiences, social networking, and other generalized approaches, make sure that some communication from top leadership is both personal and face-to-face.

Different leaders use different techniques, though most use a combination of many approaches.

Making a Personal Commitment to Your Cause

Tom Voss listened to Anita Hill's testimony at confirmation hearings for U.S. Supreme Court Justice Clarence Thomas and had an epiphany: some of the 100 AmerenUE employees in his division might be experiencing the same discomfort. He called them together the following day and assured them he wanted to know if there were problems. Now, as CEO, he actively promotes—and participates in—a wide-ranging diversity program.

One of AmerenUE's many initiatives was increasing the percentage of contracts going to minority- and female-owned businesses from 1 percent to 8.5 percent, with a goal of reaching 10 percent. The value of those contracts rose from about $6 million to more than $100 million. Voss's active support kept the ball rolling.

"We got push-back," Voss told DiversityInc CEO Luke Visconti in a 2012 interview. "Senior management questioned whether we were just being politically correct … we had everyone sign and commit to promoting a diverse workforce. I told them, 'Send me an email and tell me what you're doing in your area of responsibility.'" Not everybody responded.

"The ones that didn't respond, I called … and said, 'Hey, I didn't hear from you. Everybody in the company is responsible for diversity. If you don't get on board, it doesn't mean you're a bad person—it just means you don't belong in our company.'"

Loosen Up a Little

If you'd told Cisco CEO John Chambers around 2004 or 2005 that he would become a regular blogger, his response would have been, "Take it to the bank, that's not going to happen."

If you'd been smart, you would have bet against him. Blogging is now Chambers' primary form of communication with Cisco's 66,000 employees. A self-described command-and-control

guy—"I say 'turn right' and 66,000 people turn right"—he had
to be pushed hard to get with the blogging program.

"Once I tried it a couple of times, I got very comfortable with it.
You've got to be willing to listen and try new things," he said in
an interview with *McKinsey Quarterly*. He recognizes blogging
and other forms of social media as key aspects of collaborative
leadership—the form of leadership he now sees as more effective
than his customary command-and-control.

"The future's going to be all around collaboration and team-
work, with a structured process behind it," he said. His blogging
is both a recognition of that transformation and a calculated
method of persuading—not commanding—others to make the
transition as well. "I just show (them what's possible) and then,
cannily, it's like a virus that grows."

Chambers has more than a personal interest in video communication. Cisco, an IT industry giant, sells a conferencing system
with in-the-round cameras and special conference rooms that
reproduce the feel of being in a room together. Participants in
remote locations are able to look one another in the eye and
gather the information—the body language, the raised eyebrows,
the shrugging shoulders—that makes face-to-face communication so much more valuable than average video conferences.

Everybody Loves Face Time!

It's hardly news that most people prefer face-to-face meetings (well, at least those of us who think fast on our feet—I
like emails, myself!). But as part of its research for the video-
conferencing tool, Cisco commissioned a survey regarding
the importance and effects of in-person communication. The
Economist Intelligence Unit, which conducted the survey of
business leaders, reported the following results:

- In-person collaboration is critical to business success,
  according to 75 percent of the leaders surveyed. But
  more than 60 percent of communications don't occur in
  real time.

- Misunderstandings resulting from lack of in-person meetings present risks to major projects, according to 88 percent of the survey participants. Eight in 10 said they had experienced delays, the need for more resources, project "creep" or "shift," and other problems when in-person meetings weren't available.

- Body language and other nonverbal information in a face-to-face meeting is important in determining whether collaborators are engaged with one another and with their project—critical factors in success—according to 54 percent of the business leaders.

You can't always have face-to-face meetings with your team members. However, try to recognize situations when it's imperative to deliver a message in person. If you're announcing a merger, layoffs, the departure of a significant employee, or the filing of federal corruption charges, do it in person. Similarly, a major change in policy or direction may go over better after an in-person discussion. If you're aware of tension among team members, a face-to-face sit-down may forestall serious problems down the road.

Supervisors Possess Credibility as Your Surrogate

When the news, policy change, or problem doesn't warrant an appearance by the top command, give your key staff the opportunity to break the news. Empowering your supervisors and team leaders to communicate important messages has several benefits:

- It builds their credibility as team leaders. Employees' job satisfaction is linked to the perception of their immediate supervisor's influence. When supervisors communicate important messages, they strengthen the cohesion and sense of autonomy of their teams.

- As the person who has (at least theoretically) created the closest relationships within a team, a direct supervisor is among the most trusted of your surrogates. Allowing supervisors to disperse information helps them knit those vital collaborative relationships.

- Requiring supervisors to deal with sometimes problematic situations—including complaints about their own policies or tactics—challenges their skills and ultimately increases their leadership abilities.

- Employees are more likely to absorb news delivered by a person than announcements made by email or newsletter.

- Although top leaders should communicate with their workforce, they shouldn't overdo it. You want to maintain a little of the mystique of power—if your wife or husband says to you every day, "We need to talk," pretty soon that phrase loses its sense of import.

When having your key staff members communicate important messages, keep the following in mind:

- Give them a clear message to communicate.
- Train them to communicate effectively.
- Provide them with accurate information and, if necessary, tools to help them convey the information.

Communication Is a Call-and-Response Activity

When communication bubbles up from the bottom as well as flows from the top, your organization benefits from the perspective of employees at many different levels. The view from a ground-floor cubicle is quite different—but often just as valid— as the view from a corner penthouse office. Or, in the case of the U.S. Air Force Tactical Air Command (TAC), the view from the cockpit of a fighter jet is more sharply focused than the ground-level perspective of headquarters at Langley Air Force Base in Virginia.

It was just such an operational perspective from an Air Force pilot that pushed Four-Star General Wilbur "Bill" Creech to overhaul the military service's war strategy and training tactics.

Shortly after assuming command of TAC in the late 1970s, General Creech summoned his wing commanders and other officers to consider elements of the Red Flag combat training program. Coincidentally, he read a magazine interview with a young pilot who had recently completed Red Flag. In the article, the interviewer asked the pilot what he learned about combat from the war exercises. "I learned you can't survive in combat," he replied.

General Creech had an aha! moment. The captain was exactly right. The Air Force had been relying on a combat strategy doomed to fail, at the cost of many lives. That bit of insight from the rank-and-file led the general to overhaul Air Force tactical combat strategy.

Getting Feedback from Your Employees

Listening is fundamental to communication, and there are as many ways to listen as there are leaders to tease out what you need—not want, need—to hear. Here are some examples of ways that leaders have effectively asked for and received feedback from their employees:

- An executive VP of a major retail chain has a question for floor managers when she visits their stores: "What do you know about your customers that I couldn't possibly know?"
- The CEO of a software firm lunches regularly with employees, urging them to ask questions and offer constructive criticism. (Priding himself on his transparency and determination to engage employees, he was bemused to learn employees wanted even more openness.)

- A community college president sensed low morale within her security team. The problem? They wanted uniforms that more distinctively identified them as security. Their khaki pants and shirts didn't identify them as authority figures to the young adults on campus. (The discussion went beyond the uniforms to include issues of respect on campus—a valuable session.)

- A government agency surveyed employees regarding current strategies and then caucused to establish new priorities, set goals, and assess earlier results. The agency operates on a continuous strategizing loop of discussion, goal setting, execution, and results analysis—a good model for any organization drawing up a strategic communications plan.

Accepting Criticism Graciously

Effective leaders encourage candor and criticism. If the dead elephant in the room stinks, somebody should say so—and you should be grateful he or she did! When you're open to exchanging information and listening carefully, you will undoubtedly get negative feedback at times.

A few years ago, a dead elephant turned up in a meeting at a large hospital between the nursing staff and the director of nursing and her assistant director. The assistant ran the nurses' schedule with what the nurses considered no allowance for their preferences or occasional family obligations. She parceled out shifts on a rotation of her own design, without giving consideration to nurses' preferences for day or night shifts. She ended her report with her usual breezy, rhetorical query: "Anything else?"

To her surprise, a nurse stood up and handed both the director and her assistant a sheaf of past work schedules. The nurses marked them up to illustrate how easily the shifts could have been reassigned to satisfy the disgruntled nurses and provide full coverage of all shifts. The director listened to the explanation, perused the schedules, and then turned to her assistant and waited for her response.

The assistant appeared flustered. She acknowledged the complaints might have some validity and that the suggested scheduling could work. She agreed to reconsider her position. The director asked the nurses to appoint two people to work with her assistant, whose resolve had been softened by the shock of the public criticism.

When your organization expects and accepts candor, problems don't fester. Solutions are easier to develop. Within a few weeks, a new scheduling system was in place. The nurses were gratified to have been heard, and the assistant director had learned how to listen and respond.

Leaders No Longer Have All the Answers—or Control

In the good old command-and-control days, dictates came down from on high. In a way, this top-down approach was easier for all concerned. But it's no longer the leadership's job to come up with a solution for every problem. Instead, resolving problems now falls either to a partnership between leaders and team members or to the team with guidance from the leader.

This collaborative approach to solving problems depends on transparent communication carried out in a more relaxed, conversational style. It also depends on leadership that's comfortable letting go of unquestioned control. Adapting to that philosophy can be difficult for people who are used to having complete control of the discussion and subsequent decisions. Often, they say one thing and do another.

Take the case of a public-private business organization in Iowa whose leaders pledged allegiance to the principles of diversity, two-way communication with employees, transparent policy-making, and joint development of mutual goals. Yet, when it came time to replace its retiring CEO, the search committee put forward a pool of five candidates—all white men in the supposedly obsolete command-and-control mode. The credibility of the organization's commitment to change looked shaky. Only a last-minute intervention by a prominent (and progressive) bank leader, in the form of a critical interview given to a reporter, forced the organization to seek a wider diversity of candidates.

So here's the Golden Rule of Communication: Actions speak louder than words.

Tips for Active Listening

Active listening means paying attention to what your partner in dialog is telling you rather than concentrating on what you're going to say in response. You don't have to maintain complete silence, but you do want to refrain from unnecessary interruptions or distractions. You should also indicate that you are listening with your body language. Here are more tips for excelling at active listening:

- **Take notes.** One executive folds a piece of paper so that one side is twice the width of the other. On the wider side, he takes general notes. On the narrow side, he bullets the speaker's most important points.

- **Pay attention to the urgency or emotion of the other person's delivery, as well as the spoken content.** It helps to know your partner's behavior style (see Chapter 2) in order to accurately interpret the nonverbal messages.

- **Don't let your own emotions get in the way of what you're hearing.** Try to set aside feelings of irritation or disappointment so that you can listen without judging.

- **Verify with the other person that you have accurately interpreted what he or she has been saying.** You can do this by repeating the person's main points and asking him or her to clarify any points of confusion or disagreement.

- **When you do respond, do so in a style best absorbed by your listener.** If not, make adjustments. See Chapter 2 for tips on adjusting your delivery for various personalities.

- **Inquire what action you are being asked to take, if any, in response to the discussion.** For example, does the speaker expect you to pass the results of the dialogue to anyone else? If so, in what form?

Above all, do respond. Silence or inaction is the worst possible response when someone is trying to communicate with you. Even if you don't intend to do any of the things the speaker is asking you to do, you owe it to him to say so and explain why not. Take this advice from Robert Herres, former CEO of USAA Insurance Co.: "If employees feel like they are throwing pennies down a well and they never hear a splash, they are going to stop throwing the pennies. We have got to show them we are listening."

Getting Eggs to Fly: Facilitating Change

Chapter

4

In This Chapter

- Pulling everyone on board for the ride
- Changing behavior to change attitudes
- Making your goals attainable
- Focusing resources for high impact

One definition of a leader: someone who manages change.

Sometimes organizations make swift changes in response to crises, but more often change happens slowly, if not always steadily. As inevitable as it is, people fear and resist change. But maintaining the status quo results in stagnation in the best of times; the necessity to change and grow is even more important when times are tough. So it's a leader's job to map change, help us overcome our fears and resistance, and accept change.

The novelist C. S. Lewis described just how hard—but essential—the task of accepting change can be in a wonderful paragraph in his 1952 book, *Mere Christianity*. "It may be hard for an egg to turn into a bird; it would be a jolly sight harder for it to learn to fly while remaining an egg. We are like eggs at present. And you cannot go on indefinitely being just an ordinary, decent egg. We must be hatched or go bad."

Leaders have a number of strategies to nudge us "eggs" toward hatching, then flying. We'll take a look at five of those strategies and some examples of the leaders who used them to facilitate change.

Get Your Ducks in a Row

The whole point of defining your mission, crafting a communication strategy, and developing both internal and external relationships is to bring about changes that will achieve the goals of your organization. Now is the moment you weave those three strands together and use them as a potent instrument for change. You want everyone to understand your mission, what needs to be done to achieve it, and their part in getting it done. You're going to use your relationships and communication strategy to bring stakeholders into *alignment*.

 DEFINITION

When members of your group are in **alignment,** their purposes are integrated; they are working toward similar or mutual values or goals.

Internally, your leadership team is united, and managers throughout the organization are on board with your growth or change strategy. At this stage, your strategy calls for making sure all of your stakeholders embrace the mission and will cooperate.

Stakeholders include employees or team members, your board of directors or stock holders, possibly factions of the public, customers, and maybe members of Congress or other governmental agencies. Stakeholders may also include opponents or competitors; you will be trying to influence them as well.

Keep Your Friends Close and Your Enemies Closer

Very few of us can bring about change on our own; we have to, as the old saying goes, "win friends and influence people." As leaders, you need to pay attention to your natural allies, your "public" (workforce, teammates, customers), and your opposition.

Your success will depend, in varying degrees, on your credibility with these people.

Pay particular attention to people who have the trust of your larger audience. These influencers may be your friends or your opponents. Either way, you've got to deal with them. If they agree with you, they can be powerful allies in persuading others to accept your leadership. If they oppose what you're trying to achieve, you'll have to either convert, neutralize, or silence them.

How Much Difference Can One Person Make?

The Nike Foundation launched a worldwide initiative in 2004 called "The Girl Effect," with the aim of eliminating poverty by focusing on the welfare of girls. In particular, the foundation supports programs aiming to change the custom in some countries of marrying off very young girls in exchange for livestock or something else of value to her family. The longer a girl remains unmarried, the more education she gets and the better off economically she is as an adult.

Behane Hewan, in rural Ethiopia, is one of those programs. A partner in the program, Ato Tesfahun Wondie, demonstrated just how influential one person can be. He went above and beyond the established Behane Hewan program, gathering the 60 most influential leaders in his community for regular discussions about the roles of men and women. After 18 months, the community banned child marriages. Maria Eitel, CEO of the Nike Foundation, told Fast Company Magazine that the decision was remarkable: "That's 2,000 years of tradition ended," in large part because Ato Tesfahun Wondie involved his community's key influencers.

Influencers are especially important when you're trying to create major change or institute reform. If you're new to the organization you lead, identify influential players as soon as possible. Appoint one as your deputy, with the responsibility of acquainting you with the internal political landscape.

Embrace Your Opposition

Abraham Lincoln famously pulled his main political rivals into his inner circle after his election, naming them to the positions of Secretary of State, Secretary of the Treasury, and Attorney General. He couldn't, he said, "deprive the country of their services." Lincoln kept them on even when they occasionally tried undermining his policies.

Drafting your opposition gives you several advantages. You're blunting their criticism by involving them in the process, and you're bringing their followers into the fold, too. If, like Lincoln, you handle them deftly and sincerely, your biggest critics may evolve into true allies who substantially contribute to your success.

Getting your rivals on board may take some doing, depending on their motives for opposing your goals. Here are a few strategies:

- Hold them accountable and highlight their performance. A CEO initiated bimonthly meetings, at which managers would report and justify results to their colleagues. Naturally, the managers passed the pressure to perform to their own teams.

- Build a coalition of allies—the more influential, the better—to isolate holdouts. Depending on your organization and your goals, your allies may be elected officials, the public, or the news media.

- Demonstrate (it's better than describing) the reasoning behind your mission. Former Chicago Mayor Jane Byrne moved into a public housing development to bring attention to its high crime rates and the dangers faced by its residents.

- Pop the perception gap bubble. Requiring managers (including yourself!) to experience the same conditions as your employees or customers may reveal a picture that isn't as rosy as you think. Leaders of New York's subway system pooh-poohed complaints about graffiti, petty crime, and the smell of urine until they, themselves, were required to commute by subway. Ground your perceptions with an occasional visit to the service level of your organization.

Change Behavior to Change Attitudes

Change isn't easy, even when everyone is on board with the goal. If you've ever committed to a diet, you recognize that truth. You can minimize resistance, reluctance, or inertia by building new behavior into your organization's routine. If you want departments to coordinate and collaborate, design your structure so there's no other option.

That's what Harley-Davidson did. The company instituted a structure of overlapping team circles for projects, requiring interdepartmental communication and cooperation to design, develop, and market a product. The teams formed as needed and dissolved at the end of a project. The collaboration made the best use of the relevant talent, sometimes pulling in people who would otherwise have been sitting idle waiting for a project to reach their department. As I mentioned in Chapter 1, Harley-Davidson went to great lengths to create strong relationships among workers, so that they would be dedicated to creating quality products for customer satisfaction. The team circles contributed to that effort because workers were involved in the total project, not just their particular piece.

Think about it. What's the universal advice if you want to increase your savings? Pay yourself first, right? And even better than that is having savings taken out of your paycheck automatically, so you never see the "missing" money. Restructuring your processes so that desired behavior is also required behavior serves the same purpose as the automatic deductions—it takes away the need to think about what "should" be done. This strategy will contribute to organizational success, doubly so when opposition makes it unlikely that change will happen on a voluntary basis.

Do you buckle your seat belt? In 1983, only 14 percent of Americans did. The following year, states started passing mandatory seat belt laws, despite the public's outcry that using seat belts should be a matter of personal choice. But people buckled down and buckled up because of steep fines if they didn't. More than 80 percent of us now believe seat belts are a good thing. Forcing a change in behavior resulted in changed attitudes.

BREAK POINT

Don't delude yourself that a restructuring strategy is a one-and-done. You'll have to enlist first-line supervisors to keep up the pressure for change. Otherwise, employees will revert to old patterns at the first opportunity—just as you may reach for that piece of chocolate cake even months after succeeding at the first stages of your diet.

Achieve Multiple Goals with a Single Strategy

Your main goal may be cutting costs and using employees more efficiently. At the same time, you might want to make a point about the need for more funding from your board of directors or a public entity. Look at your goals from every angle to see how changing your organization's structure will fulfill your core mission as well as your long-term and short-term goals. Ideally, each strategy has multiple effects.

General Wilbur "Bill" Creech's mission in the 1980s was to transform the Air Force's Tactical Air Command (TAC) into an efficient, proud, deployment-ready fighting machine. As I pointed out in Chapter 1, General Creech used a variety of tactics to achieve his goals. He wasn't above exploiting TAC's weaknesses—even as he worked to correct them—to illustrate the need for more resources.

He reminded his commanders at every opportunity to stop assigning tasks when there weren't enough resources, and he restructured training to highlight—not hide—shortages in crews and equipment.

When General Creech took over, a TAC wing with 3 squadrons (A, B, and C) was authorized for 72 aircraft manned by 90 complete air crews. However, the wing actually had only 60 aircraft and 63 complete crews, spread over the 3 squadrons. The squadrons were "sharing shortages" by borrowing aircraft and crew from one another. None of the three was actually fully equipped or staffed.

General Creech put an end to the sharing. In the new structure, aircraft and crew were allotted to Squadron A, then to Squadron B until the needs of both were completely fulfilled. That left Squadron C with only 50 percent of the planes it needed and 10 percent of the crew members. The shortages were the same, but they were more obvious.

Restructuring served the general's first purpose, which was having two complete squadrons with tightly coordinated crews ready for immediate deployment. The fact that the third squadron wasn't ready increased the pressure on the general's superiors to alleviate the shortages with more resources. (By the way, General Creech became an internationally known leadership expert after retiring from the military.)

Reward the Results You Value Most

Suppose one of your values is closer coordination between your sales and marketing teams, or your development and sales departments. You're aware that kind of cooperation leads eventually to higher revenues. How do you make it happen?

Change your pay structure so that some percentage of each department's compensation is linked to the other department's goals. By enforcing collaboration, you'll be enhancing each department's success. It sounds logical, but it's not a common practice. Leaders that do connect the goals of related departments have higher rates of revenue growth or mission success.

Enterprise Rent-A-Car's leadership makes it clear to employees that customer satisfaction and loyalty are key company values, so much so that the executive team created the Enterprise Service Quality Index (ESQI) to measure how effectively each branch is building these long-term assets. The company surveys customers monthly, quizzing them on service and reliability. High customer satisfaction results in customer loyalty and, the big prize, repeat business.

Branch managers know their ESQI scores are an important factor in their performance reviews; nobody at a branch with below-average scores will be promoted. The ESQIs are as important as branch growth and profitability when it comes to assessing managers' prospects for moving up in the company. That gives them a big incentive for hiring great people and training them to provide excellent service.

The additional benefits of these reward strategies include tighter team bonding, higher employee and customer satisfaction, and increased commitment to the mission. Those valuable assets contribute to the bottom line whether you're leading a business, a nonprofit organization, a government, or even an army.

How Do You Eat an Elephant?

You eat an elephant one bite at a time.

Effective leaders manage change the same way, by breaking the goal into attainable steps and assigning responsibility for each step—that step and no more—to a specific person or group.

What may have seemed like a blue-sky goal, impossible to achieve, becomes doable.

I used the technique to raise my son on a reasonably nutritious diet which, when he was a toddler, was a daunting prospect. "Just come up with three meals for today," I said to myself. And I taught him his part, too: "Just three more bites of the salad and you'll be finished with dinner." Neither one of us worried too much about the menu for the following day. Lo and behold, he just turned 21. Together, we ate the elephant.

 FOCUS

Only ask people to achieve what's in their power to achieve. If the goal of the business district council is to improve the appearance of storefronts, and I am a block captain of the council, I have the authority to work with the half-dozen businesses on my block to make improvements. It's a level of responsibility I can handle. I won't worry about what happens on other blocks. I'm even more likely to succeed if the goal is specific—storefronts should be repainted whenever graffiti appears, for example—rather than generalized.

Police Commissioner William Bratton plugged the principle into his strategy for reducing crime in New York City in the mid-1990s, when it was considered the most dangerous city in the country. A 2004 *Harvard Business Review* article, "Tipping Point Leadership," describes how Commissioner Bratton succeeded in making the city one of the safest in the country, in part by challenging his force to make New York safer, "block by block, precinct by precinct and borough by borough."

"For the cops on the street, the challenge was making their beats or blocks safe—no more," wrote authors W. Chan Kim and Reness Mauborgne. "For the commanders, the challenge was making their precincts safe—no more. Borough heads also had a concrete goal within their capabilities: making their boroughs safe—no more. No matter what their positions, officers couldn't say that what was being asked of them was too tough ... responsibility for the turnaround shifted from Bratton to each of the thousands of police officers on the force."

Your ability to define a goal in manageable steps or segments is an invaluable tool in achieving change.

Make the Most of Your Existing Resources

Oh, boy! Everyone's in agreement with what needs to be done. Then you run up against the inevitable issue of limited funding or resources. Who gets the money? Whose project has priority? This is where many leaders falter, either spending a bunch of time fighting to get more—meanwhile, neglecting their agendas for change—or scaling back their goals.

This is the moment for creative thinking. What is your primary goal or primary problem? Prioritize, then focus on that issue.

There are two schools of thought about reducing personal debt. One way is to pay off your highest rate credit card first, then move on to the second highest, and so on down the line until you're debt free. The second approach is paying off the smallest balance first, then rolling that payment over to the next smallest bill. Either way, you're focusing limited resources in a way to make a bigger impact rather than merely making a minimum payment on every bill.

Substitute Creativity When Money Is Short

Owners of a small manufacturing company needed to grow, but the plant's operations were already exploding out of their existing space. They lacked the money to increase the size of their facility. Rather than give up, the two called a meeting of their workforce to ask for suggestions—a first for the company.

To their delight, their workers had plenty of ideas. The employees developed a new labeling and storage system for parts, rearranged machines for a more efficient workflow, and eased access by reorganizing the 400-square-foot space. The result was an additional 175 square feet of usable workspace.

Not only was the company able to grow, but employee productivity grew. The more efficient layout helped, but so did the satisfaction the workers gained from having input into solving the problem.

Reassess and Reassign Your Assets

New York's transit system was rife with crime, a situation earlier chiefs wanted to remedy by having transit police assigned to every subway line and station. When Bill Bratton took over, he didn't waste his breath arguing for the money to pay for that unrealistic solution.

Instead, he commissioned a tracking system to catalog crimes by type, location, and severity on an hourly, daily, and weekly basis. With that information, he pulled officers out of low-crime stations and assigned them to the hotspots. At the same time, Bratton deployed more plainclothes officers to keep criminals off balance about the strength of the police force. The crime statistics improved dramatically.

On another front, one of Bratton's deputies realized the transit police had too many unmarked cars but not enough office space. At the same time, the city's parole division was short on cars but long on unused office facilities. Bratton and his deputy arranged a trade. They solved both divisions' shortages without any extra funding.

By using his existing resources more effectively, Bratton got results and could lobby far more persuasively for increased funding. His success in New York was no fluke. Bratton also successfully deployed these and other strategies in Boston and Los Angeles; you, too, can put them to use.

Hire Good People

In This Chapter
- Recruiting good employees
- Building a pipeline of candidates
- Making interviews meaningful
- Bringing new hires on board in style

Hiring right is the number one factor contributing to the success of an organization, according to many surveys of business leaders. They rank it above even employee performance and achieving organizational goals. Former U.S. Secretary of State Colin Powell put it this way: "Endeavors succeed or fail because of the people involved. Only by attracting the best people will you accomplish great deeds."

Achieving that goal is no haphazard matter. It requires recruiting candidates on an ongoing basis, employing intelligent screening and interviewing techniques, bringing new team members on board in a way that ensures their success, and evaluating your hiring process to keep it up-to-date.

If you wait until you have a job opening to start your hiring process, you're falling behind in what some experts describe as a "war" to find the best employees. This chapter highlights some best practices for hiring people who have the intelligence and judgment you want, as well as the loyalty, passion, and drive to get the job done.

Creating a Culture of Constant Recruitment

At the moment, you don't have any job openings. So you're not worrying about a lack of candidates for sales jobs, engineering positions, or even members for your department's bowling team. The economy has been weak, after all; you figure you'll be flooded with applicants if a position opens up, so why bother looking before you need anyone, right? Wrong!

You know that little gurgle that develops right before the car runs out of gas, or the burp-and-sputter noise that comes from the outdoor faucet when you turn it on for the first time in spring? Those noises signal air in the pipes. In all likelihood, the car is going to coast to a stop, and the hose is going to spew brown, rusty water before it runs clear. Those aren't the metaphorical sounds you want to hear from your candidate pipeline. When you turn that tap, you want a strong, even flow of good people.

Keeping your candidate lines flowing means that you make recruitment one of your business strategies—something you embed in your organization's culture. You build it into your bonus structure, consider it an aspect of brand building, and recognize it as part of your quality-improvement programs.

Keep Your Pipeline Primed

The first step in keeping the pipeline flowing is making an inventory of your current liabilities and assets.

Liabilities are key positions that, if their current occupants suddenly left, would leave you desperate for replacements. They are mission-critical. Do you have accurate job descriptions for those positions? Have you assessed the *core competencies* needed to be successful in those jobs? One key to hiring the right people for the right job is the ability to clearly describe a position and its requirements.

DEFINITION

Core competencies are skills critical to high-quality job performance. Core competencies differ from job to job. For example, an accountant doesn't need the ability to connect easily with people, but that skill is a core competency for a salesperson.

In addition to specific skills, you want candidates who fit your company culture. If yours is a service company, you're looking for warm personalities and strong customer focus. An engineering firm wants candidates with technical capabilities or people good at problem-solving. Have you included those attributes in job descriptions?

Assets are people already working for you. When you look at the competencies and personalities required for important positions, also review current team members to see how they match up. Looking ahead to identify someone within your organization who has potential gives you time to train and polish that person.

FOCUS

"Best-in-class" companies had at least one ready-and-willing successor for 53 percent of their key positions, according to the Aberdeen Group's 2010 Strategic Workforce Planning survey of 240 organizations. In the so-called "laggard companies," the figure was 15 percent.

The best-in-class organizations had workforce plans in place in 90 percent of their divisions, compared to 15 percent for laggard companies.

Hiring from the inside is usually less expensive than seeking outside candidates. You don't have to advertise or hire a headhunter. Your inside candidate has at least some of the skills you're looking for, so training costs less. In addition, that person already fits into your culture and is familiar with your values, mission, and goals.

Turn Your Employees into Talent Scouts

Current employees are assets in another way. They are one of
your best sources for identifying potential employees. Let everybody know you're looking for good candidates and that you not
only welcome their recommendations, you're actively seeking
their help. Make an employee recruitment program part of your
business strategy. Employees recruited by your current workforce
are better suited to the job and have better retention rates than
candidates found by other methods.

Follow the example of Quicken Loans. The company converted
its entire workforce into a team of talent scouts. As a result,
almost two thirds of its new hires are recommended by current
employees. A lot of companies have formal employee referral
programs, but Quicken's is among the most extensive. Here are
just a few of the dozens of ways Quicken encourages participation, many of them considered best practices for employee
referral programs:

- **Offers contests and bonuses for finding the best or
  the most job candidates.** The contests are specific
  in their goals, time frames, and geography. Quicken
  covers the cost of taxes for bonuses and cash prizes.

- **Guarantees that the referred candidate will be con-
  tacted within a defined period, usually just a few
  days.** A quick response by the company is considered
  essential in employee referral programs.

- **Keeps referring employees informed of the hiring
  process.** Keeping them in the loop maintains their
  participation.

- **Offers training in recruitment techniques—not just
  for HR employees, but also for people the company
  thinks would be good talent scouts.** Familiarity
  with the company's hiring policies and needs makes an
  employee more likely to approach a good prospect.

- **Introduces referral programs to new employees as part of their orientation process.** A new employee, if prompted, can think of two or three other people who are considering a job switch.

A bank in Ohio created an aggressive employee referral program, with the result that almost 80 percent of its hires came from those referrals. That success enabled the bank to cut costs for agency fees from 21 percent of its recruiting budget to 3 percent. Overall, the bank saved more than $500,000 as a result of its internal referral process and other strategies. You may not hit the 80 percent mark, but many companies see big improvements in their percentage of employee-recommended hires.

Put Your Brand to Work

Use your organization's good name to sell job candidates on the benefits of working for you. Aim to be included on *Fortune Magazine*'s annual list of "The 100 Best Companies to Work For." The companies that make that list—and they're often the same ones year after year—make employee recruitment a high priority. And because they strive to be good places to work, recruitment is easier.

Ernst & Young has made *Fortune*'s list for 14 straight years. Besides boasting employee benefits that go well beyond the standard insurance package and prime parking spots, Ernst & Young prides itself on meeting aggressive recruiting goals. The company climbed 18 steps up the *Fortune* ladder, from 77 to 59— and you better believe it ballyhoos the achievement.

"We know our people and our culture power our business," said an Ernst & Young spokeswoman, announcing the 2012 recognition. "We believe our increased standing reflects a strong culture that is not just a nice thing to have—it is a competitive advantage that is core to serving our clients."

Maybe *Fortune*'s list is out of your reach, at least this year. That doesn't mean you can't tout your brand as a great employer— so long as it's true. When companies feature employees in their advertisements, they're creating the image of a good place to work. Walgreens stresses the high quality of its pharmacists in commercials. The drugstore chain isn't speaking exclusively to customers—it's also reaching out to pharmacists looking for jobs.

The last locally owned bank in Santa Barbara, California, was recently purchased by a larger banking company—to the consternation of customers. The new owners responded by running advertisements promising to continue the policy of "inclusion and respect" toward employees. The ad (which also promised continued personal, localized service) said that those policies had resulted in employee retention rates among the longest in the banking industry. The message? A good place to work is a good place to bank, and vice versa.

If you doubt the power of a brand name to evoke a workplace image, consider the problems of Walmart. For years, the company has contended with a reputation of treating employees badly—which resulted in a loss of customers. To fight that image, the Arkansas-based retailer has also used employee-focused advertisements.

Identify Your Prime Hunting Grounds

Not knowing where your best hires come from is like refusing to use GPS when you're late for an appointment in a strange city. You can cut hiring time an average of 6 percent when you identify your best sources of job candidates. Saved time is saved money. Figure out what metrics are important to your recruiting success and keep track of them.

Tracking your most productive sources and tactics is part and parcel of constant recruiting. It doesn't matter if you're small or large, you should know where you get your best leads. If yours is a tiny firm, the source for your leads could be a local leader in the know. Large companies are increasingly using computerized systems for talent management, although a tool alone doesn't make a good recruiting system.

Intuit created a custom system dubbed "The Bat Computer" to combine and analyze all manner of hiring information, including recruiter productivity, cost of hiring, the accuracy of budget forecasts, and more.

Harness Facebook, YouTube, and More

You can't ignore social media, especially if you want to reach younger candidates. First of all, have you noticed that people under the age of 30 barely use telephones? Even email is almost obsolete, withering as texting and tweeting gain primacy. If your business strategy relies on college recruiting to any degree, you need a focused campus recruiting plan that includes social media.

Ernst & Young (there they are again, with their aggressive recruiting strategy) uses Facebook extensively to reach students and student groups. The company sponsored an online contest, soliciting student videos in which they talked about their goals for a professional services career.

The company appoints recruiting teams dedicated to major college campuses. Ernst & Young, like other companies, develops and maintains relationships on the campuses. Some firms individualize their websites with different portals for different schools—adorned with school mascots and featuring school colors.

Regardless of your interest in campus recruiting, keep your websites fresh and up-to-date. Competition for candidates' attention—never mind actually getting their applications—is stiff. Your website has to be intuitive, attractive, and fast. You've got a few nanoseconds before they push the "back" button and go on to another site.

Hiring for Diversity

The need to develop and maintain a diverse workforce is a given and, in many cases, a requirement. If you're a government contractor, you're required to hire—or at least attempt to hire—ethnic minorities, women, veterans, and people with disabilities. It's not always easy. As someone who wants a diverse workforce, what do you do?

You follow a strategy I talked about in Chapter 4. Basically, it's this: Identify the results you want and make note of the behavior leading to those results. Reward that behavior. Build the rewards into the structure of your organization.

Great leaders use such a strategy all the time to meet their objectives. It's no good demanding results. When you make change worthwhile to individuals, their behavior will change and results will follow.

FOCUS

"Never hire or promote in your own image. It is foolish to replicate your strength. It is idiotic to replicate your weakness. It is essential to employ, trust, and reward those whose perspective, ability, and judgment are radically different from yours. It is also rare, for it requires uncommon humility, tolerance, and wisdom."

—Dee Hock, founder and former CEO of VISA Credit Card Assn.

Sodexo, a food and facilities management services firm, embedded the value of attracting, developing, and maintaining a diverse workforce into its organizational mission. The company achieved award-noteworthy results by explicitly stating its objectives, establishing a system for measuring results, and rewarding executives who achieved the goals. Here are some of its successful tactics:

- Executive bonuses are based, in part, on meeting the company's diversity hiring goals. Performance reviews, which determine merit raises, include a component on minority hiring achievement.

- The company developed a Diversity Index Scorecard, providing standards for measuring efforts and success in hiring and retaining a diverse workforce.

- The company listed diversity as one of its six strategic goals. Diversity initiatives were carried out not only in hiring but also in developing, promoting, and retaining minority employees.

- Sodexo established separate channels for reaching female and racially diverse candidates. As a result, Sodexo increased the number of ethnically diverse candidates by 38 percent and female candidates by 32 percent.

Staying in Touch

Some people are good at keeping in touch. President George H. W. Bush (the elder) was reported to send dozens of handwritten notes, marking significant—or not so significant—events in the lives of friends, acquaintances, and donors. You should be doing the modern-day equivalent with potential employees.

When I advise you to be on constant lookout for good candidates, I don't mean putting their names and phone numbers on a list and then forgetting about it. Constant recruiting means finding good people and developing relationships with them. Even if they aren't looking for a job right now, or you don't have a position that's right for them, keep in touch.

You probably give the same advice to job seekers—identify what you want, and then develop a relationship with the people who can help you get there. Persistence pays.

Keep in touch not only with new candidates but also those who have declined an offer in the past, those who are employed and aren't planning a move, and former employees you valued but who moved on for one reason or another. I'm not suggesting you stalk anyone, but some companies do use clever tactics:

- Send cookies and a note on birthdays and holidays. One recruiter says this works because people rethink their lives on those occasions. This soft-sell approach usually results in an appreciative phone call from a candidate who might not have responded at all if the cookies arrived on any old Wednesday.

- Once a year or every six months, invite your favorite candidates to lunch "to catch up." It doesn't hurt to have a senior manager come along to pick up the check.

- Ask your best candidates—and, by the way, many firms are now referring to recruiting as "talent acquisition"— if they can recommend some talented friends. One firm goes so far as requiring hires to cough up the names of three potential recruits before the employer will hand over the offer letter. (Not a firm I would want to work for, actually.)

People want more from a job than an income and 9-to-5 hours. They want to be engaged, a concept covered at length in Chapter 6. Employers have discovered that an engaged workforce is more productive. Engagement is based, in part, on relationships. Successful recruiters begin creating those relationships early, then work diligently to maintain them.

Screening Candidates

Every now and then, I hear a news report about an executive being forced to resign because he or she lied about qualifications or experience. This always astounds me—not because people lie, but because no one caught the lie before making the hire.

I've checked the references and employment background of several dozen candidates on behalf of a nonprofit organization that conducts national searches for executive positions. I usually finish up by saying, "Is there anything I haven't asked about this candidate that you think a hiring committee should know?" Many times the person chortles and says, "I've never been asked so many questions before on a reference check." Unfortunately, I think that's true—many organizations give short shrift to reference checking.

The organization I work for provides a template of about 25 questions. It obtains the candidate's written permission to question both listed references and other people who may not be listed. Before I start, I call the candidate to say I will be checking their references, both listed and nonlisted. I ask if there is anyone I shouldn't call at that point. I also ask if there is anything I might be told that the candidate wants to let me know about ahead of time.

Then I begin with an internet check—Google and other search engines, LinkedIn, Facebook, and a few others.

Require References and Check 'Em!

Check every candidate's references without exception. You'd be surprised at the information that turns up in a basic reference check. In one case, I didn't get beyond Google before finding out from newspaper accounts that a candidate had previously been accused of falsifying information on a résumé, arrested and charged with theft for failing to return a rented automobile, and discharged for embezzlement from a previous employer.

I've come across several instances where someone fudged their accomplishments. How did I find out? I asked the supervisor at each previous position: "So-and-so says he did this while working at your organization—is that accurate?" Well, the person might respond, "Those things certainly got done while he was here," the implication being they weren't necessarily the candidate's accomplishments. Or I have asked, "Would you rehire this person?" An answer of "no" is very telling.

I always promise the candidate and the references that I will treat their information confidentially. I don't tell the candidate who I call—even if he or she has given us the names—and I don't use names or identifying titles in the reports I give to a hiring committee. I keep the written reports straightforward—they're just summations of what each reference says in response to a question. The only opinion I offer is a brief note at the end, which is read only by the consultant running the search. Because a minimum of three people are interviewed for preliminary interviews and six or more for final candidates, the reports give an overall picture of a candidate.

Yes, past employers are constrained regarding what they can tell you about a previous employee. But they can tell you if they would hire the person again. Co-workers or former co-workers are not constrained in the same way. And you would be surprised what even listed references will sometimes reveal about a candidate—if you ask.

And that's the point: some organizations never ask. They don't call schools to find out if the person attended or graduated as he or she claims; they don't confirm employment dates or titles with previous employers, let alone call former co-workers or bosses. How crazy is that?

Prehire Testing

Behavioral tests, when used in combination with tests that indicate what motivates a person—whether it's social relevance, power, money, aesthetics, or something else—can be very useful in determining whether a candidate is going to fit into your corporate culture or your leadership team. There are also tests that evaluate a candidate's core competencies, which can be vital if you're looking for a certain set of abilities.

Test results are not definitive by themselves, but you can use them to supplement the impressions you get from in-person interviews and talking with previous employers. The results are especially helpful when evaluated by a skillful, experienced professional. If you don't want to pay to have all candidates for a job evaluated, consider screening the top three candidates.

Preparing for the Interview

Behavioral interviews are the best way to evaluate a candidate's skills and experience. Rather than asking "what would you do" in a certain situation, a behavioral question asks, "What have you done?" These kinds of questions prompt a candidate to give examples and anecdotes. The best indication of what someone will do in the future is what they have done in the past.

Questions in behavioral interviews are based around core competencies needed for the job the candidate is seeking. Since a person's behavior patterns don't change much over time, this kind of question indicates how that person is likely to respond to similar situations in a new job.

Behavioral questions can't be answered "yes" or "no." The interviewer doesn't want answers based on theory or philosophy. The questions are specific, and the answers should reveal the actions of the candidate.

BREAK POINT

The three most meaningless job interview questions are:

- Where do you want to be in five years?
- What is your biggest weakness?
- Why did you leave your last job?

Behavioral questions are open-ended. They usually start with phrases like:

- Tell me the last time …
- How did you deal with …
- Give me an example of …

If you're trying to determine whether a candidate has leadership ability, you might ask:

Have you ever had to resolve disagreements between team members? How did you do it? Were the disagreements legitimate? Did you have to take one side or another? Why were you the one to solve the problem?

If the job requires customer-service skills, behavioral questions might be:

When was the last time a customer got angry? What were the circumstances? How did you handle the complaint? What was the outcome? Was the customer satisfied? Is he still a customer?

Checking Core Competencies

Every job requires critical competencies, but not every job requires the same competencies. You'll be more successful teasing out a candidate's suitability for a job if you've thought about the core competencies required for that position. Compose questions ahead of time that revolve around those skills. Another approach is to require candidates to take standardized core competency assessments.

This list covers several of the major competencies. Create interview questions that reveal a candidate's abilities in the areas important to you.

- Organizational skill
- Analytical ability
- Ability to work in teams
- Flexibility
- Reliability and work ethic
- Customer service focus
- Leadership skills
- Oral and written communication skills

Prepare a list of questions for each position you want to fill. You might even note typical responses and what those responses tell you about competency. While your list of questions may be long, you don't have to ask every one of them. But ask each candidate identical questions for a fair comparison of their answers.

FOCUS

Sometimes hiring the right person doesn't mean hiring the person with the most experience or the longest résumé. The best person may be the candidate with more ability than experience. Skills are teachable, quality is innate.

Be ready with follow-up questions, or reworded versions of the original, in case you aren't satisfied with the answer. Keep the interview focused but conversational. Use your questions as guidelines, not a strict script. Don't be so distracted by your next question that you don't pay attention to the candidate's response!

You can find many websites that provide examples of behavioral questions. Search for "behavior-based questions" and the core competency you're seeking in an employee.

Decide whether you will conduct the interview alone or have a panel of questioners. From the candidate's point of view, a group interview may seem more conversational. He or she isn't forced to parade from one person to another for individual interviews. From the interviewer's point of view, less leadership time is wasted, follow-up questions flow more easily from the panel, and the group can more easily reach a consensus since they are judging the candidate from a situation in which they are all participants.

On-Boarding New Employees

Have you ever gotten a new job and found yourself twiddling your thumbs the first several days, anxious to be doing something but not sure what it should be? New employees shouldn't be left to their own devices—they want to be successful. It's your job as a leader to make success easily attainable. You can't take a "let 'em sink or swim" attitude.

The new jargon for employee orientation is "on-boarding." On-boarding is a comprehensive process of welcoming new employees, familiarizing them with company culture and policies, making expectations clear, and explaining how results will be measured. Effective on-boarding programs result in higher levels of productivity from a new employee in a shorter time, a faster feeling of success, and higher rates of employee retention.

On-boarding starts almost imperceptibly the first time a prospect visits your website. If it's a good website, it conveys your organization's values, vision, and mission. Your prospect begins getting a picture of your culture and clues to the core competencies required by the job he seeks.

Hospitality is how you greet the new employee. You want her to settle in as comfortably as you want a guest to settle into your home. Provide what she needs—a security badge, if one is necessary; a computer that's ready to go; instructions on how to use the phone system; business cards; someone to show her where the bathrooms and cafeteria are ... you get the idea. These are the little things, the elements that help someone make the transition from job candidate to employee as comfortably as possible.

The employee orientation facet is how you introduce someone to the company cultures. Ideally, this is a team effort with both formal and informal aspects. You go beyond showing the new guy how to use the copy machine (that's important but falls under hospitality); you're letting him know company values. Maybe you encourage employees to volunteer by giving them time off to do so; you may want to stress your employee referral program or let them know the values violations that mean immediate termination.

On-the-job training is your structured program for managing the new employees' first 90 days on the job. They learn what you expect from them, how—and how often—their work will be evaluated, what support systems are available, and when and how they will be trained.

Successful companies have structured on-boarding programs that pay for themselves many times over. Yet one HR study revealed that 80 percent of companies do a poor or mediocre job of bringing new employees on board. Another study found that employees who participate in a formal process are 58 percent more likely to be with the organization in three years than employees who aren't on-boarded (which should have no resemblance to being water-boarded).

Your on-boarding program should be consistently structured, but it doesn't have to be identical to those offered by other organizations or even between two of your own new employees. The program may vary, depending on the position. Here are some elements to consider:

- A development plan for that employee, which may give short-, medium-, and long-term objectives.

- Discussion of communication and behavior styles of the new guy's colleagues. Doing so may help him fit smoothly into the operation more quickly.

- Meetings with key people inside your organization and important clients or outside contacts.

- An overview of personalities, relationships, and idiosyncrasies that affect how work gets done. Don't descend into gossip.

- A conversation with new employees asking them how they like to be managed. You may not entirely agree, but the discussion will at least give you insight into the person's behavioral style—at least from his or her point of view.

As a team leader or organization executive, your participation in the on-boarding process is important. Effective leaders from every realm report that personally presenting some part of the orientation message conveys to new employees that they are valued by their leaders.

Don't drop the ball. Make periodic evaluations and follow-up sessions part of the 90-day on-boarding process.

A great employee who sticks around is money in the bank.

Work That Matters

In This Chapter

- Creating meaningful and engaging work
- Distinguishing between engagement and motivation
- Cultivating and increasing employee engagement

People want to feel that they are part of a cause bigger than themselves, no matter whether they work for the armed services, a business, a university, the city's sanitation services, or a professional sports team. And they want their employer to acknowledge their contribution as making a difference.

When we make a difference, we're happier. We work harder. We're energized by the challenge and the sense of belonging. Our self-confidence increases. We're proud of what we do.

"Oh, sure," you're thinking. "That's fine if you're a doctor, a rock star, or winner of the Nobel Peace Prize. What about the little people—the office clerks, garbage collectors, and grocery store baggers?" It's the same for everyone: if you can see the larger picture of what you contribute to society, you're more likely to be committed to your job. Have you ever been to a city where the sanitation workers are on strike? If so, you know they contribute mightily to the civility of daily life.

If you can inspire that feeling of contributing, you're on the road toward achieving your goal as a leader. Rather than employees who carry out their duties because you say so and they have to, you have a team committed to the broader effort. When you build commitment, your team will show more initiative and creativity. As the late Green Bay Packers football coach Vince Lombardi said, "Individual commitment to a group effort— that's what makes a team work, a company work, a society work, a civilization work."

Meaning Is in the Mind of the Beholder

Here's an actual blog exchange between anonymous strangers about their work, illustrating the difference between someone who finds meaning in work and someone who doesn't:

> "Let's face it, most jobs/careers are meaningless and unimportant. I have such a hard time coming to terms with the fact that I'm never going to do anything really important," wrote the first man. "I am basically nobody and always will be."

And here is another man's response to that post:

> "I clean toilets for a living. I could tell you that I hate it, that cleaning up after people is no fun and quite repetitive ... I excelled academically and like to think of myself as quite intelligent. Yet, I clean toilets. ...

> "Now, let me give you the other side of things. I get to work with my wife every day. I get to provide a service that truly helps busy families keep their lives together. ... Most of us spend most of our time at 'work,' so it is vitally important to find some measure of meaning or value there."

He then describes taking the time to do extra, unpaid cleaning to surprise a client who gave birth to her first child on the day he and his wife were scheduled to clean.

"We did something really nice for a couple of new parents so they could spend time with each other and their new baby, instead of worrying about taking care of mundane pursuits. We did the mundane, but turned it into something exciting for all. ... and here I am, still just 'cleaning toilets' for a living."

Employee Engagement Is an Emotional Bond

Commitment and pride in work—the force that prompts people to go beyond what is expected—is called *engagement*.

 DEFINITION

Engagement is a combination of competency and passion for work. Engaged employees are intellectually absorbed and challenged by their work. They are intent on performing to the best of their individual ability in order to achieve their organization's goals.

Boiled down, engagement is largely about relationships, challenge, and self-respect. People want to see the effect of their work on their customers, their company, and their community. They want to connect with people at work who care about them. They want the opportunity and tools to do their best work. They want the chance to learn to do even better work. And they want someone to appreciate all that they are accomplishing.

Engagement is the emotional foundation of success. When you cultivate engagement, you're investing in your employees' psychological well-being as well as the success of your company.

The Difference Between Engagement and Motivation

Although engagement is related to motivation, it isn't the same. *Motivation* is the will to do what needs to be done. That will is supported by an external factor—often referred to as the carrot or the stick. A person is motivated either by reward or punishment. An engaged employee is much easier to motivate because he cares about the task itself, not the potential reward or punishment.

Psychologists break motivation down into three distinct components:

- **Activation:** The decision to do something.
- **Persistence:** Sustained effort to achieve a goal despite obstacles.
- **Intensity:** The concentration, energy, and resources spent in pursuing the goal.

To Motivate or Engage?

Employees may be motivated to do something, but it might not be the something you, as leader, have in mind. You have to get them going, and in the direction of the organization's mission. To do that, you have to find the motivation—the reward—that moves them in the direction you want them to go.

Engagement is a weave of positive emotions and the state of being absorbed in your work so that you don't need to be spurred to action. You are continually involved—a good sign that you are engaged is when you sit up in bed at 3 A.M., wakened by a sudden insight into your current project. You are still motivated by a reward, but the reward is the challenge and satisfaction of solving a problem.

"Engagement" implies a continually active mind—one involved in problem solving, able to create an unexpected solution.

FOCUS

"After a certain point, money is meaningless. It ceases to be the goal. The game is what counts."

—Aristotle Onassis, Greek oil tycoon (Easy for him to say!)

Some management theorists now view "motivation" negatively, as a form of manipulation in which offering a "reward" for doing something means the work isn't worth doing for its own sake. Eventually, these theorists argue, the system of rewards kills interest in the task; in the meantime, an engaged worker is intrinsically interested in the job, regardless of reward.

I see their point, but most of us think of motivation in more general, largely positive terms. Besides, there is some value to being "manipulated" by a reward. I'm usually engaged in my writing, but sometimes I still need the motivation of a deadline to get it done!

In 1968, Professor Frederick Helzberg identified what he called the primary "motivators" of worker satisfaction: responsibility, achievement, advancement and growth, recognition, and the work itself.

Responsibility Lightens the Load

Do you like it when someone stands over you and tells you, minute by minute, how to do your job? Probably not. Neither does anyone else. The ability to control some aspect of your job fulfills the need for self-direction. Knowing that your employer trusts you to act responsibly also contributes to your job satisfaction.

As a leader, you demonstrate trust and recognition of value when you give employees increased autonomy. In turn, the employees are more likely to trust and respect you because you ceded responsibility. They are energized by their sense of self-control, belonging, and value.

The sanitation department of an East Coast city had problems with weekly trash collections being completed on time. If a route wasn't finished by the end of the day, workers quit and went home anyway. The sanitation workers were widely perceived as lazy.

Their union leader negotiated a change in policy. Workers could go home as soon as they finished their route, even if it was before their shift ended. Granted the responsibility for managing their own time—and goaded by their leader to change the union's public image—the sanitation workers made it a point to finish routes early and leave.

Input Multiplies Commitment Fivefold

Giving people choices, rather than just issuing and enforcing rules, increases their commitment to the goal by a factor of 5 to 1.

I didn't make that up. In a famous experiment, psychologist Ellen J. Langer—now a Harvard professor—gave lottery tickets to half the participants while allowing the other half to choose their own lottery numbers. Then she offered to buy back the tickets.

Logically, the two groups should have demanded the same amount of money for their $1 tickets. But people who chose their own numbers—in results replicated many times—consistently required five times more for their tickets than those who held randomly issued lottery numbers.

In another study, Langer and a colleague demonstrated that nursing-home residents who made more choices in their daily routines and had responsibility for watering a plant became more active. They reported being happier. Eighteen months later, the death rate for those residents was significantly lower than the overall rate for residents of the facility.

The relevance to leadership is obvious: if you want increased commitment, give people a voice in defining and designing their own roles in a project.

Advancement + Growth = Achievement

A kindergartener learns to tie his shoelaces and feels great about it. He's mastered the final detail of his job—learning to get dressed. Two weeks later, tying his shoelaces is a routine matter; he does it well, but it's not worth bragging about. His next big accomplishment will be the day he rides his bike without training wheels. That achievement will remain satisfying until he starts itching for the car keys.

I rewrote that paragraph about the kid and his shoelaces several times. I fiddled with the wording. I considered whether the example makes my point clearly. I was pleased with the verb "itching." I feel good about that paragraph because I'm confident of my expertise in leadership and the writing skills I've developed over 30-some years.

Achievement, challenge, and mastery of a skill are all elements that create engagement. Very few people are satisfied with mastering one skill and repeating it without variation for the rest of their careers.

Effective leaders recognize the importance of ongoing training and education. Allowing us to develop expertise and use it to work on increasingly difficult challenges is an important factor in keeping us engaged.

 BREAK POINT

A word of warning: don't encourage people to develop expertise and then prevent them from using it—that's just frustrating.

This "Drug" Has No Bad Effects

Recognition, achievement, and self-esteem are high up on the list of primary human needs, right after food, shelter, and love.

When we perform well, we want to bask in acknowledgment of our achievement. We want that pat on the back. On the flip side, when things are going badly, we hope someone cares. We want the pat on the back to turn into a helping hand. We don't want to be the worker in the cubicle who dies at the desk and isn't discovered for a week!

Here's a little secret about recognition, reward, and praise: they are like drugs. In fact, they produce a drug in our brains. We get a little pulse of dopamine when something pleasant happens—like receiving kudos from the boss. And as a side effect, that dopamine surge reinforces our desire to repeat the behavior that caused it. We become more productive because we're looking for another hit of dopamine.

 FOCUS

Offer praise five times more frequently than you hand out criticism. This ratio of 5 to 1 is the "sweet spot" for giving an appropriate amount of positive feedback. It's true of any relationship, including friendships and marriage.

Psychologist John Sottman discovered what he called this "magic ratio" of positive to negative interactions while studying factors that contribute to divorce. Sottman said he could predict, after one brief conversation with a newlywed couple, whether they would be divorced in 10 years, based on their ratio of negative to positive interactions in those 15 minutes.

It doesn't take much to give recognition that promotes pride. A supervisor in a not-for-profit community college organization emailed reminders to her crew about how to correctly do fact-checking of résumés. She started with this sentence: "I would like to thank all of you for your diligent and timely efforts during the past months ..."

More importantly, she ended with this sentence, putting a sometimes tedious task into the context of a broader mission: "Thank you for your important work. Your reports help shape the future of higher education."

If you live by the mantra that "no news is good news" or "if I don't say anything, you're doing fine," forget about it! Given a choice, the human brain favors a negative interpretation over a positive one. When you say nothing, the brain doesn't think everything is fine. It begins muttering, "I must be doing something wrong." Silence is especially destructive when praise is expected for a job well done—dopamine levels don't remain level, they drop. It's like not getting a cake at your birthday party.

Give Praise in a Language the Recipient "Gets"

Remember Steady Eddie from Chapter 2? He wants praise in the form of a quiet word over a cup of coffee. The Social Influencer, on the other hand, would prefer a Mardi Gras party. Written recognition is essential for some, meaningless to others.

Remember: it is the responsibility of the person delivering a message—in this case, praise—to deliver it in the form preferred by the recipient. If the recognition or reward isn't given in the preferred form, the person being praised might not even realize he or she has been praised. It's up to you to deliver recognition in the way best suited for each individual.

 BREAK POINT

Employees who don't get enough praise or feel their boss doesn't listen are 30 percent more likely than other workers to suffer a heart attack and three times more likely to seek another job within a year.

What's worse than no praise, or praise that isn't in the form you prefer? Praise that isn't specific. Or praise for something that isn't particularly noteworthy. False, insincere, or undeserved praise doesn't produce that little surge of satisfaction we crave. Recognition we earn is the best kind.

Contrary to popular myth, you can give too much praise. An over-the-top ratio would be 11 positive feedback statements for every negative statement. But don't worry about being overly generous. No one is. In fact, only a third of employees report being praised by their boss in the previous seven days. The glow we get from recognition and reward is very short-lived. We should be giving or getting positive comments—a simple "thank you" counts—every day. Once a week is pretty stingy.

Taking the Pulse of Employee Engagement

If engagement is so important, how do you know if your team has it or has enough of it? Luckily, engagement can be measured.

In the mid-1990s and continuously since then, the Gallup Organization (yes, the same one that does public-opinion polling) interviewed thousands and thousands of workers all over the world, in almost every industry, and at levels ranging from the bottom of the employment ladder to the top. The "motivators" identified 30 years earlier were still valid, but the goal was to create a manageable survey tool that pinpointed key components of engagement and enabled researchers to put a number on their findings.

The result was a 12-statement survey (called Q12) in which employees are asked to rank, on a scale of 1 to 5, how strongly they agree or disagree with the statements. The collective answers are analyzed to produce a composite rating of that group's level of engagement. Only Gallup can administer Q12, and the organization doesn't allow reprints of the questions (though they are readily available online), arguing that the real value of the survey is the interpretation of results and comparison with its databank of responses that Gallup provides.

Millions of people and thousands of companies use similar surveys. The U.S. Army measures the "climate" of service units and the effectiveness of leaders with its own 12-question survey.

Federal employees are periodically given an even longer list of questions, also focusing on conditions that encourage engagement. The surveys all assess the level of pride in the workplace, trust in leadership, and opportunity for individuals to contribute to an organization's goal. In the following section, I include a survey that you can use in your organization. (Again, while using the survey is valuable, there is additional value in having your firm's results compared to the results of similar organizations.)

Work and Well-Being Survey

This survey, used by leadership consultants to the technology industry, is typical of workplace engagement surveys.

These 17 statements are about how you feel at work. Read each statement carefully. Please rate each question as to whether you strongly agree (1), agree (2), are neutral (3), disagree (4), or strongly disagree (5).

1. I like coming to work each day.

2. I respect the people I work with.

3. I believe I am using my potential wisely.

4. The company offers ample opportunities to share my thoughts and ideas.

5. The company treats me as a person first and an employee second.

6. Communication within the company is conducive for me to do my job well.

7. Leadership communicates the vision, purpose, and direction of the company.

8. I clearly understand what is expected of me.

9. I understand and feel good about my contributions to the company's success.

10. I feel I am fairly paid for my contribution to the company.

11. At appropriate times, I receive a "way to go" for a job well done.

12. I have the proper training to exceed the company's expectations of me.

13. I am provided the opportunity to learn and grow.

14. My co-workers are committed to doing quality work.

15. The company uses internal technology and systems that support my efficiency.

16. I respect and trust the top leadership (ownership) of the company.

17. I intend to be here one year from now.

You say your company is too small for such sophisticated evaluation tools? Maybe so. But you can use the questions for gathering information without conducting complex mathematical assessments. Even without statistical analysis and extensive "debriefings," you gain critical information you can use as a leader.

Surveys like this are meant to guide actions. Feedback isn't useful without a response. If one of your values is accepting—and acting on—input from team members, this is where your blue jeans meet the saddle. As one researcher puts it, the questions and answers are "remedial." In other words, the results shouldn't be filed away in a drawer. They are meant to be discussed with the aim of increasing engagement.

A low score on a particular issue is a cue to work on that topic. Have a departmental meeting and discuss the high scores and the low scores. Ask what needs to be done. Then do it, as far as it is feasible and with participation by those who were surveyed. Without action, the collection of opinions contributes to a well of cynicism and frustration. Don't relegate valuable information to the dark hole of apathy.

Engaged Employees Make Your Business Better

You care, of course, because you have integrity based on your values. But if you need another reason to care, here it is: organizations with an engaged workforce have better business results. That holds true for government agencies, private corporations, public institutions, and the armed services.

By better results, I mean higher profits, higher sales growth, and higher productivity. Safety records are better, with far fewer accidents. Companies whose workforces aren't engaged have turnover rates half again as high as companies with engaged employees. Those employees take fewer sick days and are much less likely to quit for a job someplace else.

The internet's vast virtual libraries are filled with studies demonstrating correlations between employee engagement and healthier-than-average bottom lines. There is no evidence that better financial figures are the direct result of an engaged workforce, but there is general agreement that the elements of engagement do influence success. Low employee turnover, for example, saves money in training new employees. High employee satisfaction is linked to higher-than-average customer satisfaction, which in turn increases profits.

The more engaged—absorbed, challenged, and stimulated— your employees are, the more likely it is that your company will prosper.

Lead 'Em, Don't Assault 'Em!

>>> **In This Chapter**

- Making a psychological contract with followers
- Bolstering positive leadership
- Emphasizing strengths rather than focusing on weaknesses
- Enriching jobs, granting autonomy, and retaining accountability

"You don't lead by hitting people over the head—that's assault, not leadership," said Dwight D. Eisenhower, 60 years ahead of his time in describing what is now considered the most effective leadership style for creating an engaged workforce.

Positive leaders are good at managing themselves, staying calm in a crisis, and adapting goals to changing circumstances. By keeping themselves motivated and focused, positive leaders engender confidence and stability among their followers. They'll do what they can to create a positive atmosphere for their troops; one newly appointed CEO famously took down the barbed wire fences that literally surrounded the financially embattled corporation he'd been hired to save.

Positive leaders emphasize making the best use of people's strengths and skills rather than focusing on and trying to fix their weaknesses. They establish clear goals for an outcome, but they'll let their team members decide (within limits) the best way to achieve the goals. They offer challenging opportunities, building their own strengths and the strengths of others the same way you build muscles in a gym.

Setting the Tone for Mutual Respect

A healthy organization starts with an atmosphere that encourages people to take initiative, accept responsibility, work together toward a shared purpose, and experience satisfaction that goes beyond their paycheck. As a leader, it's your job to create that positive climate, balancing the needs of your people with concern for the bottom line. While salary and other conditions are spelled out in a written agreement, the *psychological contract* that governs the human relations aspects of a working relationship is usually unspoken.

 DEFINITION

A **psychological contract** is an unspoken agreement between an employer and employee regarding their mutual expectations of one another. The employer commits to treating the employee with respect, compassion, trust, and fairness and, in return, the employee responds with hard work, loyalty, and commitment.

Positive leaders are more likely to openly discuss their view of the psychological contract, letting employees know how they can expect to be treated in the workplace. Increasingly, psychological contracts require leaders to relinquish some measure of control over workers. Positive leaders can handle this prospect, but less capable leaders fear letting go will result in chaos.

Dee W. Hock urges you to flirt with chaos. By encouraging, not resisting, the desire of others to exercise authority, make decisions, and take initiatives within the bounds of clearly established principles and defined goals, you're creating an atmosphere in which innovation and human satisfaction flourish.

He knows a little something about leadership and letting go. As founder of the Visa credit card association, Hock decentralized operations at every opportunity. Now retired as Visa's CEO, he promotes a concept he calls "chaordic" management, referring to systems, businesses, or organizations that are neither rigidly ordered nor chaotic. They require a new understanding of the relationship—the psychological contract—between leaders and followers.

"The word 'leader' presumes followers," writes Hock, a member of the U.S. Business Hall of Fame. "The word 'follower' presumes a choice …. If the behavior of either is compelled, whether by force, economic necessity or contractual arrangement, the relationship is altered to one of superior/subordinate, manager/employee, master/servant, or owner/slave. Where behavior is compelled, there you will find tyranny, however benign."

Positive Leaders Are Okay with Loose Reins of Control

Whether or not they're familiar with the chaordic concept described in the previous section, today's most effective leaders practice what Hock preaches:

- They're lifelong learners, concentrating on managing themselves as much as others.
- Their organizations are geared toward providing rich working environments as well as rich stockholders.
- They're flexible; they can adapt quickly if there is a crisis or if a strategy isn't successful.

"The first and paramount responsibility of anyone who purports to manage is to manage self," says Hock in his essay, *The Art of Chaordic Leadership*. "It is a complex, unending, incredibly difficult, oft-shunned task. We spend little time and rarely excel at management of self precisely because it is so much more difficult than prescribing and controlling the behavior of others."

Create a Positive Atmosphere for Growing Success

One of the first things a positive leader does is create an environment conducive to accomplishment. This isn't an issue of space and décor, though surroundings do matter. Most psychological contracts call for a climate that encourages innovation, with the realization that there will be occasional mistakes or missteps. Fear of failing should not be a factor.

That seems obvious. Believe it or not, there are still people who practice fear-based leadership. Here's a textbook example of characteristics of a fear-based, command-and-control leadership style:

- Sets standards that may be impossible to meet
- Often demands projects or tasks be accomplished in the way she would accomplish them
- Communicates in an abrupt manner; has been known to scold, demean, belittle, and humiliate people in meetings
- Is insensitive to the human aspects of managing people

This is a vivid illustration of how not to create a positive environment. By demanding control, this leader created chaos. Hired as a "change agent," she achieved a few of her goals in a five-year period. But she created an atmosphere of institutional chaos that was publicly chronicled and drove away some of her best executives. Her worst trait, according to both supporters and detractors, was insensitivity to fellow humans.

"To her, people are a resource on the same budget line, with the same value, as chalk."

Accomplishing Change Is Easier in a Positive Climate

Campbell Soup Co. also hired a new CEO as a change agent in 2001 to turn around its failing fortunes. Besides various financial and market ailments, the company's workforce engagement scores were among the lowest ever measured. The new CEO,

Douglas Conant, made improving the dismal climate his top priority. He dubbed the effort "Campbell's Journey."

- He paid attention to complaints about previous management missteps.
- He formed personal relationships with as many workers as he could.
- He took note of the fearful atmosphere, which included rumors of a takeover, and made immediate efforts to ease the tensions.
- Most importantly, he acted on his observations.

First, he took down the barbed wire fence that snaked around the company's campus in Camden, New Jersey. Physical surroundings are important, and there's not much positive about barbed wire.

Within the first 18 months, Conant fired 300 of the company's 350 executives—a strong response to complaints about the company's previous years of mismanagement. He replaced many of them with insiders, which also improved morale.

He demonstrated his philosophy of building trust through personal connections by acknowledging employee achievements with handwritten notes, as many as 10 a day. He put on his sneakers when he had a spare moment and walked the halls talking to people. Conant appointed a group of employees to establish Campbell's Promise: "The company values its people, and its people value the company."

"To win in the marketplace," Conant says frequently, "I believe you must first win in the workplace …. Once you earn people's trust, you have permission to do some amazing things."

It wasn't a recipe for instant success. Improvement was slow for the first three years. But by the time of the 2008 economic crisis, when other packaged goods companies experienced average drops of 25 percent in shareholder returns, Campbell's figures rose 7 percent.

Positive Leaders Adapt in a Crisis

Nimble leaders with a positive bent of mind don't let catastrophe defeat them. They reassess and adjust strategy. An important characteristic of a leader is his or her ability to remain composed in the face of crisis.

By letting their teams know what changes are being made and why they are necessary, positive leaders help workers maintain belief in the future.

At Campbell Soup, a less self-confident leader might have been tempted to indulge in self-pity when faced with a recession that threatened company progress. That didn't happen at Campbell Soup. The CEO metaphorically shrugged, then kept to his mission. "That's the challenge ... that's what makes it exciting. When the challenge gets bigger, you have to pick your game up a notch."

FOCUS

Positive leaders follow the philosophy inherent in the Chinese belief that the word *crisis* is interchangeable with *opportunity*.

P.S.: Sometimes It's Okay to Be Authoritarian

Command-and-control leadership is archaic, outdated. That's true, insofar as that leadership style is based on a belief that workers are lazy and will do anything to avoid their duties. But there are rare times when elements of authoritarianism are appropriate.

In a crisis, when time is short and immediate action is required, a leader may step in and issue orders without input from team members. The leadership of Harley-Davidson, which became known for its participatory leadership style, first turned the company around with a very traditional top-down recovery strategy.

When all team members are new or inexperienced, a leader may impose assignments or a strategy, either as a means of getting things done or as a training exercise. A crew of unskilled workers, especially if they have no real interest in the job, may also require an autocratic leader.

Ideally, you cede authority and responsibility to others with the aim of enriching their work lives and developing future leaders. But ultimately, there's the old Harry Truman line: "The buck stops here." That gives you final responsibility and, when necessary, the final word.

Focusing on Strengths, Not Weaknesses, Enhances Success

You already know that an engaged worker is a more productive worker. One sure way to increase engagement is by designing work that lets people use their best skills and knowledge as much as possible.

Letting people do what they do best increases their self-confidence, and therefore their effectiveness, satisfaction, and productivity. That's common sense backed up by plenty of research. The Gallup Organization's decades of worker engagement studies reveal the odds of employees being engaged are only 9 percent when leadership fails to focus on their strengths. By contrast, when an organization does acknowledge and invest in its people's strengths, the odds of engagement are 73 percent.

Some experts advocate designing jobs so that 75 percent of an employee's day involves activities that use his or her best skills. The result is greater professional productivity but also maximum personal growth and satisfaction.

Does Everyone—or Anyone—Recognize Their Strengths?

By the way, not everyone knows what their best skills are (probably because so many organizations have focused on fixing weaknesses). One of your tasks may be helping people identify their strengths. If no one has ever done that, or asked what they believe their strengths are, this process in itself can be very gratifying. After all, it's a form of praise to say, "Hey, did you realize you are the best in the department at Task XYZ?"

Behavior and core competency assessments, such as those mentioned in Chapter 2, are one way of determining an individual's strengths. The reports often spell out how to capitalize on strengths and avoid falling into the pitfalls of weaknesses. Some companies make these tests available to all employees.

And there's always that old standby: ask your employees or team members what they are good at. Ask them what their interests and hobbies are; you may find they have applicable skills that you didn't know existed.

Satisfaction Is Rooted in Expertise and Achievement

Psychologist Frederick Herzberg identified factors that contribute to a worker's job satisfaction and affect the way people feel at work. His list of motivators, first compiled in 1959, are factors that meet an individual's psychological needs to feel valued. (They overlap, somewhat, with factors that contribute to engagement.)

- Achievement
- Recognition
- The work itself
- Responsibility
- Promotion
- Growth

In addition to identifying work motivators, Herzberg developed a framework for enriching jobs to make them more intrinsically satisfying.

> **BREAK POINT**
>
> Job enrichment should be meaningful. It's not enriching, for example, to tell someone who is fastening 10,000 bolts a day to increase his or her output to 20,000 bolts. Nor is rotating a variety of meaningless tasks, like washing floors one day, scrubbing toilets the next, and fanning the boss every third day. Adding a challenging task and increasing responsibility are two ways to enrich a job.

When you combine your knowledge of a person's strengths and your awareness of how the motivators work to create a more fulfilling job, you serve both your organization and your employees. You're giving them opportunities to find meaning in their daily activities while creating workers who make significant contributions to your organization's mission. That's the essence of strengths-focused leadership.

Enrich Jobs by Adding More Challenging Tasks

Aligning tasks with individuals' special abilities and skills is a first step. Positive leaders are dedicated to continual learning, both for themselves and those they lead. Put this philosophy in action by making sure your workers get opportunities to develop their strengths even further.

By now, you know the importance of frequent, positive feedback in creating engagement. You also learned in the previous chapter that giving people discretion in deciding how to achieve a goal is more effective than spelling out every step of the process. Now it's time to address the last three motivators on Herzberg's list: responsibility, promotion, and growth.

Simply put, enriching a job is a three-step progression:

1. Increase expertise

2. Increase autonomy

3. Increase authority

I explore each of these steps in detail in the following sections.

Everyone Benefits When an Employee's Expertise Grows

People thrive when they're acknowledged as experts. You can increase their skills over time by adding challenges to their work, providing them with mentors who oversee their growth without stifling their initiative, and sending them to seminars or industry meetings that expose them to the latest advances in their field. As their expertise develops, give these people special assignments or specific tasks. Make them responsible, start-to-finish, for projects in their areas of expertise.

Ask them to report their results up the ladder of authority. You'll be up-to-date on activities. They get the glow of knowing their work is appreciated beyond their own department.

Don't forget to call on them to design new products or projects. By developing their expertise, you're creating internal engines of innovation!

Reward Increased Ability with More Responsibility

Autonomy is an initial step in the progression of increasing responsibility. That could be as simple as letting an individual schedule his or her own time, control some resources without requiring sign-off by a supervisor, or report results directly to a management committee.

Another way to increase responsibility would be requiring your experts to mentor less-senior people, helping them develop expertise. Increased expertise and increased autonomy, when responsibly handled, obviously will lead you to giving that person increased authority for making decisions and allocating resources.

This positive, strengths-focused approach is the most effective way of leading people who are motivated by achievement. And people who are motivated by achievement are going to be your most successful team members. They're looking for opportunities that fulfill their need for flexibility, challenge, autonomy, and responsibility.

Money Isn't Everything, If You Have Enough to Live

People get more satisfaction out of doing a job well than they get from money or other material compensation. An inadequate salary can cause dissatisfaction, but a poor salary isn't usually the factor that causes the most dissatisfaction at work. In one survey of people who left their jobs, unsatisfactory pay came in fifth.

Money is one of what Herzberg called "hygiene" factors (which have come to be known as *dissatisfiers*). These are things that meet your basic work-survival needs: decent pay, acceptable administrative policies, good working conditions, and a reasonable relationship with supervisors and co-workers. The absence of these things causes irritation or dissatisfaction. But they're rarely, if ever, going to rise to the level of defining your satisfaction with work.

As a leader, you do have to both provide motivators and meet the "hygiene" needs of your team.

The issue of pay is a good example. When your work is challenging but the pay is unfairly low, you can't concentrate because you're constantly worrying about bills. If the pay is outrageously good but the work is mind-numbing or your boss never, ever notices your contributions, eventually you become depressed, cynical, or lazy.

As Wisconsin consultant Rob Bell puts it, "Appreciation is a gift to employees. Compensation is their right."

You Can Fail But Still Prevail

In This Chapter

- Responding to mistakes
- Taking responsibility for mistakes
- Putting your organization's good above your own

Even highly competent people make mistakes. A bad idea, a carelessly executed strategy, simple immaturity, or lapses of integrity—they've all been known to play a part in failures of leadership that damage or sink an organization.

Why do some leaders falter or fail when things go wrong, while others survive and even thrive? The reasons are rarely simple, but they usually relate to the basic principles of leadership: adaptability, integrity, human relationships, communication, and responsibility.

Leaders succeed in the face of failure when they accept responsibility, adapt their strategies, and focus on the good of the organization. They encourage maturity among team members when they respond to honest mistakes with compassion. Great leaders learn from their mistakes and let others learn, too.

On the other hand, those who cry "not my fault, not my responsibility" and try, at all costs, to protect themselves are less likely to survive a mistake. Leaders who pervert their principles bring disaster down not only on themselves but on their organizations, too.

Adaptability and Laser Focus on Goals Save a Doomed Crew

Polar explorer Ernest Shackleton could have been exhibit A of leaders whose careless decisions condemned his 27-man crew to an icy death. Intent on reaching the Antarctic in 1914, Shackleton hired inexperienced adventurers for the expedition, brought along untrained sled dogs for the planned trek across the continent, and, most arrogant of all, ignored warnings that heavy ice packs had built up, making successful passage an unlikely and treacherous proposition.

Instead, Shackleton is held up as an example of great leadership. After his ship, the *Endurance*, became trapped in the ice, Shackleton made it his mission to save every one of his crew. Although he had been sloppy in planning the expedition, he made up for it with an extraordinary focus on survival after disaster struck. It took two years, but he succeeded in saving his men. The catastrophe forced the arrogant explorer to hone the skills that now define leadership:

- He redefined his mission, demonstrating adaptability to changed and changing conditions. Okay, it would have been better if he'd adapted earlier, but at least he learned this lesson eventually. As conditions worsened, Shackleton continually adjusted his strategy, moving his men from the ship to an ice floe and then to an island before setting off himself to find a rescue team.

- He demonstrated confidence and a calm demeanor. When efforts to hack the *Endurance* free of the ice failed, Shackleton didn't show "the slightest sign of disappointment," according to the ship's doctor. "He told us simply and calmly that we would have to spend the winter in the (ice) pack."

- He established a structure of routine and shared responsibility for the crew, keeping them occupied and even entertained. And because he ignored class and rank distinctions, Shackleton created a team of equals. He enforced standards of behavior to ensure the team members remained unified.

In short, Shackleton embodied his mission to save the members of his organization, a mission he described succinctly in his journal: "I pray God, I can manage to get the whole party to civilization."

Mistakes Teach Great Lessons, If You're Willing to Learn

Willingness to admit a mistake and take responsibility for the results is such a paramount leadership trait that Harvard University asks college applicants to answer the question: "What have you learned from a mistake?" Shackleton's story is instructive, in part, because of his own contributions to the disaster that befell the *Endurance*.

Many well-known leaders have failed, learned from their mistakes, and reinvented themselves. Steve Jobs, founder of Apple Computer, was fired from that company in 1985, largely because his leadership qualities didn't match his genius for invention. Twelve years later, a matured and somewhat mellowed Jobs returned to Apple and, of course, led the company to greatness.

The failure hit Jobs "like a brick in the head" but turned into a life-altering event. "The heaviness of being successful was replaced by the lightness of being a beginner again, less sure about everything. It freed me to enter one of the most creative periods of my life."

Expecting Perfection Sets the Stage for Failure

You set performance standards to provide a high bar for achievement. But striving for perfection or insisting on excellence in every detail is not realistic. If you do insist on perfection, your people will be afraid to make a move without your explicit approval. That's counterproductive.

Set the expectation of good, consistent performance. Let your people know you appreciate their honest efforts, even if results sometimes fall short. Rest assured, there will be setbacks, failures, and mistakes, despite your team's best efforts to avoid them.

FOCUS

Reward risk-takers, even if they fail. The biggest successes require trial and error. If you praise only those who succeed, no one will be willing to risk failure by trying something unorthodox or innovative. Showcase the efforts of people who stick their necks out and try something new.

Because you have clearly communicated your standards, you'll be able to recognize the difference between a genuine mistake and one caused by recklessness or by chronic indifference. Treat them accordingly.

Respond Compassionately to Honest Mistakes

Robert Bell's first job was as a gopher at Dick's Supermarket in his hometown. A shy teenager, as he tells the story now, Bell came out of his shell with the encouragement of the people at Dick's. Gradually, he asked for, and they gave him, more responsibility.

He knew he'd reached a new pinnacle the day he was allowed to make the daily bank deposit.

On his way to the bank, Bell looked around and realized the two bank bags weren't in the car. Panicked, he stopped, got out, and discovered one of the bags on the roof of the car. The other was nowhere to be found. After a frantic search of his own and another with the help of the store manager, Bell realized the money was irretrievably lost. He went into the store's office to face the boss, sure he would be fired.

Instead, the boss declared him responsible from that day forward for making the daily deposit "because no one is going to keep an eye on the bank deposit like you will."

His boss's compassionate response to a youngster's mistake benefited them both, says Bell, author of *Beyond Paper or Plastic—8 Items or Less to Remarkable Service*. By allowing the boy to learn from an honest mistake, the boss taught Bell lessons in leadership as well as responsibility. The boss reaped his reward in loyalty. Bell remained with Dick's Supermarkets, Inc. in leadership roles for more than 25 years.

Acknowledging Failure Is a Strength

FedEx, the overnight delivery service, sells trust. The company promises to deliver your most important possessions safely and swiftly to their destination. Employees pledge to nurture that trust with the company's Purple Promise: "I will make every FedEx experience outstanding."

Which is why a security video showing a FedEx delivery man heaving a boxed computer monitor over a fence caused quite a stir. Posted on YouTube, it was seen by more than 800,000 viewers and picked up by several television stations.

"What got into the mind of that young man, I'll never know," FedEx CEO Fred Smith said later in a magazine interview. "There's one thing pretty simple in our business: You don't throw or drop a package. That's pretty basic."

FedEx apologized. And not just to the customer. FedEx posted its own video, calling the incident "absolutely, positively unacceptable" and acknowledging company-wide embarrassment. "This goes directly against all FedEx values," said the senior vice president featured in the video.

The company went further. It used the original video as a training tool for the rest of its 255,000 employees, who were "mad as hell" that their reputation could be endangered by one person's actions. Using the incident as a platform for learning also fits the company value of exposing, not hiding, mistakes.

Smith puts it this way: "You've got to use failures as an opportunity to improve."

How should you respond to a mistake?

- Don't yell. Remember, great leaders manage their emotions and remain composed.

- Praise publicly, but punish (or chastise) privately.

- Discuss the error. Schedule a meeting with the employee, after asking him or her to reflect on the mistake in preparation for the meeting.

- Review what you would have liked or expected to happen under the circumstances. Discuss how the situation that led to the mistake could have been handled differently or more successfully.

- If warranted, dole out consequences relative to the size of the problem. A straightforward punishment is more effective than an angry tirade.

- Don't hold a grudge. When the punishment has been enacted or the trust re-established, treat that person with respect. If respect or trust isn't warranted, the person should be let go.

Put Your Organization First

If you're a thoughtful leader, you'll dole out consequences for mistakes and manage troublesome situations in proportion to their cause and magnitude. Don't treat every problem or mistake as though it were a world-ending catastrophe.

An administrator at a small northwest college was successfully negotiating the professional ropes, advancing from professor to dean, then to a VP position with the likelihood of further promotion not far in the future. Then a new chancellor arrived, one with a more structured management style than her predecessor.

The VP resisted her approach. After a discussion, he agreed to a reassignment with reduced responsibilities and curtailed influence.

The chancellor could have fired the VP or banished him to a meaningless position. But he had done nothing wrong, he merely wasn't aligned with her managerial vision. She recognized his valuable ability to forge genuine relationships. She gave him responsibility for community development, something that was both needed and fit with his inherent people skills.

The VP was no dummy either. He reflected on his role in the organization and came to terms with his new position. He did an outstanding job with his new duties, markedly improving the school's reputation as well as burnishing his own. When he applied for the presidency of another college, his boss provided a sincerely positive recommendation.

Both demonstrated a good leader's self-awareness, and both put the school's good ahead of their own comfort. The chancellor reaped the benefits of the VP's skills while creating a position that helped him grow as a leader. By adapting and focusing on his new mission, the VP increased his credibility. The school and the community were the ultimate beneficiaries of their good leadership.

Three Strategies for Ensuring Spectacular Failure

The right way to respond to a mistake or failure may not always be obvious or easy. By now, though, the wrong ways should be fairly evident. Here are three strategies for maximizing the damage done by a troublesome situation:

- Pretend the problem never happened.
- Point fingers. Blame someone else.
- Look out for your own best interests. Forget about (or pervert) the organization's values and members.

Follow these practices diligently and catastrophe will catch up
with you. The disaster train may be late arriving but it will pull
into the station sooner or later.

Dirt Under the Rug Always Rises to the Surface

The photograph was poignant: workers carrying off the life-size
statue of legendary Penn State football coach Joe Paterno, his
right arm extended to point the way. Literally in the last months
of Paterno's life, his reputation for principled leadership crum-
bled after it became evident that the coach played some part in
covering up years of child abuse by one of his assistants.

Paterno wasn't alone among college administrators in turning
his face from reports of the abuse. But because his was the face
most associated with the glory days of Penn State football, he
will endure as the symbol of its deepest disgrace. Why, as reports
and testimony reveal, did these leaders ignore mounting evidence
of terrible crimes against children, committed by a long-standing
employee?

They did it, apparently, with a perverted sense of the good of
the organization (the third failure strategy I describe in the pre-
ceding section). Penn State administrators made a collective
decision—conscious or not—to protect the reputations of the
school and its winningest-ever football program rather than to
protect children. Whatever the details, the result was an attempt
to hide the problem.

Why didn't it work? Because hiding a crime at the expense of its
victims was a violation of the organization's values (not to men-
tion public values). Great leaders and great organizations embody
their values, they don't negate them. Doing otherwise is a failure
of integrity.

Why Are You All Picking On Me?

Crude oil gushed into the Gulf of Mexico, spilling from a rup-
tured oil rig owned by BP, the British oil firm. Eleven men were

killed when the rig exploded. The toll in environmental and financial damage mounted by millions every day over the months that the spill went unchecked. BP CEO Tony Hayward felt the pressure to staunch the flow.

He couldn't help but vent his irritation with the unfairness of it all. "What the hell did we do to deserve this?" he asked his executive team a week after the explosion. He followed up that remark with the observation that, after all, the spill was "relatively tiny" compared to the "very big ocean." As the disaster dragged on, his remarks took on a petulant air. "There's no one who wants this over more than I do," he whined in an apology. "I'd like my life back."

 BREAK POINT

"Most people, when directly confronted with proof that they are wrong, do not change their point of view or course of action but justify it even more tenaciously …. Yet mindless self-justification, like quicksand, can draw us deeper into disaster. It blocks our ability to even see our errors, let alone correct them. It distorts reality, keeping us from getting all the information we need and assessing issues clearly."

—Carol Tavris and Elliot Aronson in *Mistakes Were Made (but Not by Me)*

Great leaders don't whine in the middle of a crisis. If, as in the BP spill, the lives of others are endangered, they don't complain about the inconvenient disruption in their own lives caused by dealing with a catastrophe. They shouldn't begin finger-pointing and evading blame at congressional hearings, as BP executives did.

In all likelihood, BP was doing the best it could to cap the gushing oil well. The matter of blame and responsibility for the underlying causes of the rupture will take years to determine. What is certain is that BP, personified by its CEO, did not display either the self-awareness or the sensitivity to others that characterize true leadership.

The Dark Side of Leadership: Company Culture Decays

Leadership books, including this one, talk a lot about a leader's ability to embody the vision, values, and mission of an organization. Notice I said the vision, values, and mission of "an organization," not "of the leader." There is a big difference.

The word *organization* means that the vision, values, and mission collectively belong to the organization's members. It means that those people have a voice in articulating and carrying out the vision, values, and mission. When the mission becomes corrupted, the members have the power to object. They may not do it often, but they do have that power.

An organization is in danger of failing when leadership hijacks the rights of the organization's members. The most extreme modern example is the Enron Corp., which some scholars have compared to a cult. When Enron failed, it not only wiped out the savings of many of its employees, it also threatened the national economy.

Enron executives, masters of charismatic leadership skills, built a culture that emphasized pushing the limits in pursuit of profit. They let their own ethics erode, and then they led the rest of their organization into corruption. The message from leadership was "profits at all costs."

Enron executives used the same strategies and language that leadership gurus advocate. They pushed employees to be independent, aggressive, and innovative, and to perform beyond the call of duty. They encouraged "Enronites" to devote themselves to the organization. Enron had a 64-page company code of ethics; executives gave it lip service and ignored it in daily practice. Breaking rules was acceptable, even desirable, in pursuit of their own enrichment.

Employees Are Obliged to Stop a Leader Who Causes Harm

Very few people at Enron raised red flags. They had been robbed of their ability to offer *constructive dissent*.

Successful leaders encourage responsible followers—people able and willing to speak up when they see something going wrong. At Enron, employees gave in to *destructive consent*, standing silently by as the company was led astray.

 DEFINITION

> In their book *Organizational Leadership,* John Bratton, Keith Grint, and Debra L. Nelson define **constructive dissent** as legitimate advice and criticism from followers that keep leaders from making mistakes or limit the damage from mistakes. They define **destructive consent** as the inertia of followers in doing nothing to prevent injury to the organization from the effects of a leader's bad decision.

Constructive dissent, according to British leadership expert Keith Grint, occurs most often in organizations in which leaders recognize their own limitations and expect their followers to compensate for those limitations. But how to make that happen? Here are some examples:

- In World War II, Winston Churchill set up a communications loop that bypassed his generals so they couldn't filter negative news from the front.

- At Exxon Corp., employees are reminded twice a day about their "obligation to intervene." Regardless of rank, seniority, or position, an Exxon worker is required to speak out if he has any qualms about the safety of a procedure. If the worker encounters any resistance or delay, he's taught to utter the phrase "obligation to intervene."

- The American Foreign Service Association annually recognizes foreign service officers who have the "intellectual courage" to object to policies they believe could be harmful. The organization has been presenting "Constructive Dissent" awards for 40 years, though there are years when no winners are selected or even nominated.

So far, no one's developed a formula for guaranteeing constructive dissent. But there's no disagreement that dissent is necessary: organizations that don't allow dissent, like Enron, are much more likely to fail. Those that do allow constructive dissent are more profitable. Think of constructive dissent as leadership quality control.

Building Team Leadership at Every Level

>>> **In This Chapter**

- Sharing common attributes, not just tasks
- Building complementary strengths into executive teams
- Taking advantage of informal teams and influencers

Leadership is becoming less about an individual person and more about process.

Literature, history, and the arts put a lot of emphasis on individuals as great leaders, but few leaders truly work alone. Leadership has become a team operation. This is especially true in the twenty-first century for two reasons. First, organizations are increasingly complex; one person can't do it all. Second, the cultivation of engaged workers all but requires delegating responsibility to teams.

What makes a good leadership team? What personality types or skill sets are required? What are the benefits of team leadership? What are the drawbacks? How does the team leadership model work?

In this chapter, I address those questions by looking at executive-level teams and the transformation of the traditional pyramid structure of organizations to a framework that resembles a map of the stars. I also highlight the effectiveness of informal networks, in which members hold no official power but exercise considerable influence.

A Team Isn't Just a Group of People Working Together

A team, first of all, is defined by the existence of relationships among members. They recognize a common identity and relate to one another in ways that maintain that group identity. Team membership may be designated by management, but until members establish their relationships, the group is likely more of a task force than a team.

A team has a common purpose that goes beyond completing a task. The team defines its purpose and develops the approach to achieving its goal. Although a work group merely carries out directives from above, a team has a strong voice in defining a problem, the solution, and the means of achieving the solution.

Expect decisions to take longer within a team because of the need to build consensus. However, that front-end delay will often be offset by quick execution made possible because the team has already dealt with the whys and the wherefores of a particular decision.

FOCUS

Allow teams to create their own agendas for defining their challenges and creating the solutions. The result is more success in achieving your overall mission. As British author Keith Grint says in *The Arts of Leadership*, "Leaders are most likely to be successful when they reflect the problems straight back to where they have to be solved … at the feet of the followers."

Team members have complementary skills. They may not initially know everything they need to know to solve a problem. A hallmark of a team is the ability of its members to learn and develop capabilities as they work. Make sure you provide the resources they require to do what needs to be done.

Teams are accountable for maintaining the well-being of the group and its members, as well as accomplishing a task. They create a structure to guide their collaboration and a process for resolving conflicts. Creating and enforcing these standards encourages the growth of trust among the team members.

Co-workers on small teams tend to be very loyal to one another. With just five or six people working together, members don't want to let one another down. They're also quick to rally around one of their colleagues if he or she has a problem at work or at home.

Teams Are More Than the Sum of Their Parts

When a team is clicking, the effect is transformative. You may have seen it happen with your child's sports team. One week they're a scattered gang of third graders playing a game you hardly recognize. The next week they're high-fiving and can't be stopped.

By creating teams, you're creating engaged workers. You already know engaged workers are more productive by many measures. To take it a step further, British researchers have found that tightly knit teams, especially those with a strong commitment to the organization's objectives, are like engaged workers on steroids. Team members thrive on one another's energy, turbo-charging their efforts.

Because team members share responsibility, their ability to make good decisions is generally higher than the abilities of the individual members. A certain amount of constructive dissent adds to the quality of the decision-making. The synergy also leads to more creative problem-solving. Teams are the proof behind that old cliché, "The whole is greater than the sum of its parts."

Bringing Harmony to Your C-Suite Team

All the individual leadership traits we've talked about—integrity, vision, relationship skills, discipline, and ability to communicate—are necessary and valuable on a team. The more of them you possess individually, the better leader you are or will be.

But everyone has gaps. Effective leaders recognize their own gaps and appoint others to fill them. Leaders with the most comprehensive skill sets still need supporting casts. Very few organizations of any size have a single leader anymore. Having just one person in the lead isn't feasible and, even if it were do-able, it's not desirable.

For one thing, there's the irrefutable fact of mortality. We all hope to retire rather than expire, but it's nice for an organization to have backup in case the unthinkable occurs. Do you want an executive team whose success depends on one individual?

Assembling Your Team Based on Complementary Abilities

You pull together a leadership team by first knowing yourself—your strengths and your weaknesses. Next, you build the team by augmenting and complementing your abilities. Like other teams, yours at the executive level needs a shared identity, a common purpose, and enforceable standards of collaboration and behavior.

Review your leadership style from Chapter 2. Are you a Restless Driver, with a creative vision of the future; a Compliant Analytic, with the attention to detail necessary to execute a plan; a Social Influencer, concerned with relationships that contribute to effective collaboration; or a Steady Eddie, with a devotion to process and strategy?

Successful teams include a mix of all four leadership styles, so that all strengths are represented. A group dominated by one type or another won't be well balanced. The team's effectiveness depends, in large part, on everyone remembering the golden rule of communication: it's up to the person delivering information to communicate in the style preferred by the person receiving the message.

Developing and Managing Your Executive Team

There's no recipe for an effective C-suite team. Unless your organization is brand new, you probably won't get to assemble your dream team from scratch. In all likelihood, you'll inherit all or part of the previous leader's cabinet. So you start by working with the available "ingredients."

Crafting an executive leadership team can be a slow process. You might fire a few outright stinkers, but if you'd like to replace others, first take the time to assess their talents and see if they'd be better suited to another position where their skills won't be wasted and they just might be happier.

 FOCUS

Teams are evolving organisms. The synergy that works in one situation might not be as strong under changed conditions. A new person may change the dynamics; a new crisis may alter the group's focus. The team should be as adaptable as you are.

Whether your team is new or has been working together for years, now is a good time to launch an ongoing discussion about what leadership means in your organization. Is it stagnant? Are you, as top-tier leaders, doing any mentoring? Are you pushing the workplace initiatives that would contribute to your business strategy?

Hire someone to conduct behavioral and motivational style assessments of each member, and report everyone's results back to the group. Yes, to the group. That should start a great conversation.

A Dysfunctional Team Can Produce Sour Results

Relationships of all sorts do sour, with negative results. That's true of dysfunctional teams as well. If a team hasn't created enforceable standards—or can't enforce its standards—its sense of common mission may fall apart.

Turf battles or irreconcilable disagreements about priorities might block progress on a task or cause decision-making to come to a halt. That's why it's important to agree on a process, from the start, to avoid or resolve an impasse.

Another potential problem occurs when one person or faction of the team develops too much influence. If that happens, and the team starts discouraging diverse opinions, the team loses the value of synergistic thinking. In the worst cases, like Enron, everybody follows mindlessly behind the influential faction even to the detriment of the team's mission.

Avoid these pitfalls by emphasizing understanding and communication among team members. Pat Summitt, head coach for the University of Tennessee Lady Vols basketball team, stressed the value of shared understanding in her book, *Reach for the Summitt*. "When you understand yourself and those around you," she wrote, "you are better able to minimize weaknesses and maximize strengths."

Creating a Company-Wide Team-Based Structure

Team identity rarely happens in a vacuum. Solid relationships of trust, shared accountability, and responsibility take time to gel, particularly when many of us matured in traditional, top-down organizations. The necessity of actively pushing development of team trust and understanding is especially pronounced when it comes to spreading team-based leadership throughout your organization.

A team-based organization is grounded in the principles of employee partnership, equity, accountability, and ownership, also known as *shared governance*. In plain English, shared governance results in everyone feeling that their input has been considered in decisions that affect them. Leadership responsibilities are held by the group rather than by a few individuals.

 DEFINITION

Shared governance is a framework that promotes collaboration and shared decision-making and accountability among various groups in an organization. Shared governance is a specific commitment to decentralized decision-making that gives everyone a voice in issues that affect their work.

Changing the ideal of leadership from focusing on individuals with extraordinary talents and charisma to a structure with decentralized authority is a massive cultural change. One academic says that managing the evolution "is a universal struggle" requiring extensive planning to overcome the bias toward the "myth of the heroic leader."

Ironically, it's the "heroic leader" who must commit to changing the culture if shared leadership is going to take root. A leader has to step back in order to let others lead themselves. If he feels indispensable, he might not be enthusiastic about creating the necessary atmosphere for change. (Research shows that female managers practice shared leadership more often than males.)

Tap Your Organization's Informal Teams

Most organizations have what might be called a hidden network of stars. They're people who are influential not because of their title but because they get things done. And they get things done because of their relationships with others like themselves. These are the influencers I talked about in Chapter 4. Just as you want to get them on board when you're initiating change, you should also be aware of them in your day-to-day operations.

How do you identify these influencers?

As it happens, social scientists can map influence in your organization just as geneticists can map your DNA. The process is called an *Organizational Network Analysis (ONA)*. Essentially, an ONA is a diagram of relationships that reveals how people communicate within an organization.

 DEFINITION

An **Organizational Network Analysis (ONA)** is a map of otherwise invisible webs of information flow. You can create an ONA map by asking each person within a team or department who he or she turns to for information needed to get work done. Draw each person as a circle and each communication link as an arrow indicating the direction information flows. An organization's ONA diagram is often strikingly different from the corporation's formal organizational chart.

Think of a box of Tinker Toys, with its round node connectors and sticks. On an ONA map, each person is a node, and that person's relationship with another person is a stick or a line. Some people may be connected to others by just a few sticks. Others might be virtual porcupines, with connections coming out of them in all directions.

An ONA map gives you insight into formal and, more importantly, informal connections and teams. You may be surprised by what an ONA map reveals. You may discover hidden stars, people with extensive connections that amount to influence. On the other hand, the ONA map might help you realize that someone you had considered to be a star is actually an obstacle that others try to avoid.

The map is a useful tool. Perhaps you didn't realize Paul in production is an essential communication node; what will the people who depend on Paul do if he leaves? You need to make sure the hiring pipeline has potential replacements. You see that Jim in marketing fields communications from all over the company, even though he, himself, doesn't reach out to many people at all; this may explain why Jim is having a hard time getting his work done. You might note that no one identifies the IT department as a frequent contact; does this mean IT isn't doing its job? A map can help you decide the most effective leader for a particular assignment or whether an employee would benefit from special training. It may reveal why interteam collaborations are successful—or not.

Don't try to take over your hidden teams, but by all means take advantage of them.

Harley-Davidson Test-Drives Team Leadership

Command and control was the rule at Harley-Davidson in the 1980s, when the iconic American motorcycle manufacturer seemed to be nearing the end of the road. New ownership seized the handlebars and safely steered the company to prosperity. Employees, spurred by the crisis, were highly motivated.

With stability restored, the executives realized that the company needed a different kind of leadership to maintain employee commitment. As I noted in an earlier chapter, they ditched the command-and-control hierarchy for a fluid, team-based structure. They gave every employee responsibility for sustaining the company rather than passing ideas, problems, and complaints up the ladder.

At Harley-Davidson, executives passed leadership responsibilities to natural work groups rather than explicit teams. The so-called "circle organization" was based on three company processes: creating demand, producing product, and providing support. Company executives initially served as mentors, coaching decision-making rather than making the calls themselves.

The idea was to bring "the right people together at the right time" to work on a particular project. Harley-Davidson wanted decisions made as close as possible to the work affected. The change in leadership style meant trusting employees on the floor to make the right decision. Developing that trust, the Harley-Davidson team realized, meant providing people with ongoing education. Harley University now offers more than 100 classes. It became an organization devoted to ongoing learning—a factor that contributes to an engaged workforce.

Harley-Davidson suffered some setbacks, but the executive team persisted, unions cooperated, and the circles took shape. Harley-Davidson's leadership style evolved from lone rider to leader of the pack.

Developing Leaders of the Future

- Filling your pipeline with internal candidates
- Identifying future leaders early
- Growing your leadership trees

Leaders chosen from within an organization are more successful than outsiders. With that in mind, you should be constantly combing your ranks for high-performance candidates. In fact, you should have three prospects in development for every high-level position, according to one expert.

Identify these people early in their careers. It takes 6 to 10 years to prepare them adequately for a top-tier job. Developing leaders is like raising a child; they mature intellectually with experience. Expose them to increasingly challenging positions so they'll be better able to deal with complexity.

Your leadership selection process should be rigorous, not haphazard. Get an assessment system in place to identify candidates' adaptability, self-awareness, and ability to think strategically, as well as their operational experience. Without a system, the tendency is to hire a successor in the image of the beloved retiree or, when replacing a failed leader, someone exactly the opposite. Neither approach guarantees success.

Act Now! Avoid the Coming Leadership Crisis

Can you give me the names of three people likely to lead your organization 10 years from now? No? Don't worry, you're not alone. Nearly half of the biggest U.S. companies are in the same boat, with no working succession plan for replacing their CEOs.

They've let their leadership pipelines of up-and-comers run dry. That in itself is a failure in leadership. The global complexities of the world demand leaders who are more prepared than ever, not less. As it is, two out of five new CEOs fail in their first 18 months on the job.

Granted, you're probably not running a multinational corporation. No excuses! I use examples from the corporate world because that's the focus of most published research. (Although the U.S. Army's *Small Unit Leadership Handbook* covers a lot of the same ground.) But you can apply the concepts to mom-and-pop shops (you'd be surprised—or maybe not—at their leadership scuffles), nonprofit organizations, public agencies, and the military.

So what can you do to avoid a crisis in your organization?

FOCUS

It's never too soon to tag potential leaders for development. Colgate-Palmolive begins assessing new employees' leadership potential during their first year. Other companies like to start grooming as early as when the candidate is 30. It takes 6 to 10 years to gain the skills and experience necessary to step into the executive suite. Don't wait until the current occupant shows signs of retiring. You can't afford to dally.

First, identify your existing high performers. Internal candidates are almost always preferable to outsiders. They know the company culture, and you know or should know them. Internally grown CEOs have better track records at keeping their jobs than outsiders.

Assess their existing capabilities and areas of weakness. Devise a plan that builds on their strengths while filling in the gaps. Expose them to experiences that build their ability to think strategically in complex situations.

Create a Diverse Portfolio of Emerging Talent

Trolling for talent is a continual process. Use any tool you have.

Don't make the common mistake of identifying only clones of your current leadership. It's human nature to gravitate to people with traits similar to our own, but that's no way to pick a leader. By looking only for clones of current leadership, you're more likely to overlook people with significant potential without even realizing what you're doing. That narrow approach makes for a shallow talent pool.

If you're creating a team leadership network, you may already be gathering valuable information with behavioral, core competency, and motivational assessments. Have you checked your international offices? They could be the source of out-of-sight, out-of-mind talent.

Commission an Organizational Network Analysis (ONA; see Chapter 9 for details) and examine the junctures that indicate people with high influence and extensive connections. Those are two key attributes for emerging leaders, especially since leadership is evolving toward a collective process or network rather than individuals.

High-Potential Candidates Are Like Gold

Competition for leadership talent is intense. Training and keeping leadership prospects is—and should be—a major element of your organization's business strategy.

As a rule of thumb, you need three ready prospects for each top executive position. Count 'em. If you don't have enough, you may have to turn to outside candidates. "High-potentials," as some companies call their prospective leaders, are treasured assets.

Proctor & Gamble, a paragon of succession planning, maintains a blue binder called the Talent Portfolio. Executives track, evaluate, and compare each of the approximately 120 people in the binder twice a year on the basis of financial reports and leadership capabilities.

"Today I could show you the next generation of successors to current leaders, the generation after that, and the generation after that," the company's global human resources officer told *Fortune* magazine.

Senior managers at Colgate-Palmolive must maintain 90 percent of their high-potentials or be dinged on compensation. Don't even think of recruiting at Colgate, which has a tiered development program. Any time a high-potential hints at leaving, the company's executive team is notified and immediately swings into action to persuade the person to stay.

Helping High Achievers Reach Their Potential

Now that you know who your high performers are, how are you going to help them achieve their potential? How will you prepare them to face the future, when it's changing so rapidly?

Start with the Boy Scouts' motto: be prepared.

Create your own training handbook of fundamental skills and experiences that your future leaders will need if they reach the executive suite. Colgate-Palmolive and Proctor & Gamble include these elements in their training programs:

- Assignments with escalating responsibility and visibility throughout the organization. Sometimes called "breakthrough experiences," the assignments should be meaningful. Don't bother wasting anyone's time on mindless rotations on a fixed schedule. You want to see evidence of ability to collaborate across departmental boundaries, financial acumen, creative problem solving, and success in employee engagement.

• Formalized learning. Many organizations have their own "universities" or training seminars especially for potential leaders. Some prospects pursue an MBA or other business degree while working.

• Relationships with coaches or mentors. These people can share their wisdom and insights as your candidates navigate their paths.

• Performance standards for evaluating and tracking progress. Create your own talent portfolio of candidates so you know where they are, what they've accomplished, what else needs to be done, and how they compare to your other prospects.

Don't limit your efforts to a select few. Team-based leadership is the way of the future. Make every employee a leader as part of a strategy to prepare for collective leadership. At the very least, you'll have a more engaged workforce.

Aha! Moments: Develop Your Capacity for Adaptive Thinking

As you probably know, an aha! moment is the flash of insight you get when something that has bothered or stymied you suddenly makes sense. It's the moment of clarity that changes everything instantly. Like when you were learning to ride a bike and suddenly you got it.

Emerging leaders should experience aha! moments during their breakthrough experiences. Those are moments that expand their capacity for adaptive problem solving, according to Harvard professors and researchers Robert Kegan and Lisa Lahey. The "breakthrough" occurs when a person, stymied by a challenge beyond his or her capacities, realizes the need to think outside the box.

"The box," in this case, is the person's own way of thinking. If he or she pushes through the frustration, looks at the problem a different way, and solves it, there's an aha! moment. The person's perspective changes to allow different, more complex thinking.

Pulled by ever-more-difficult problems to solve, Kegan says our thinking progresses from one stage to another. Along the way, we're honing our capacity for strategic thinking, collaboration, our tolerance for ambiguity, and our ability to lead. We become more self-confident and more willing to trust our own judgment.

Making Succession Planning a Priority

The problems and solutions facing leaders today are like the digital cloud—invisible but all around us, always shifting and lifting. You want agile leaders prepared to operate in that atmosphere. If you're going to remain aloft, you need to make succession planning a significant part of your business strategy.

By definition, the strategic approach means that in addition to your executive team, your board of directors must be involved in the leadership development program. According to Ram Charan, author of *Boards That Deliver*, that's how it should be, since board members are ultimately responsible for the welfare of their organization and selecting its CEO. Board involvement in choosing future leaders is necessary whether your organization is a multi-billion-dollar corporation, the local art museum, or a charity running a homeless shelter.

Here's how one global corporation wove leadership development into its strategic planning efforts, after discovering its existing plan was gathering dust in file cabinets.

Shortly after its yearly review of company initiatives, the executive committee meets with high achievers and managers from every business unit to discuss and develop the part each division will play in meeting the coming year's goals.

A few months later, they all meet again. This time, they evaluate the progress of emerging leaders to match their assignments to business goals. And yes, the emerging leaders attend and participate, too. Finally, the same people meet for a third time to develop budgets.

Weaving leadership, business, and budget development together exposes prospective leaders to the process of strategic planning. They also get face time with the company's executives, who use the opportunity to familiarize themselves with their own future replacements.

Actively engaging the high achievers lets CEOs observe them in their natural habitats.

Five Must-Have Qualities for Leaders

When selecting potential leaders, look for these five attributes. They are critical for success in the twenty-first century, although they cannot be taught, only learned:

- **Self-awareness:** The essential characteristic that is the foundation of all other leadership capabilities.
- **Learning agility:** Global volatility and technological innovations require an ability to learn and adapt to constantly changing conditions. Without learning agility, skills and experience rapidly become irrelevant.
- **Comfort with ambiguity:** Many problems today don't have one cause or one resolution. Innovation requires taking risks that may cause negative results or failure. The ability to proceed without a certain outcome is an asset.
- **Ability to engage:** Leading others depends, in large part, on relaxing control while maintaining authority. Engaged workers create engaged customers.
- **Ease with collaboration:** Progress or innovation is more likely to be the result of team or network efforts. Fluid leadership enhances the collaboration necessary to get things done.

Involve the Board

Your board of directors should also be spending time individually with prospective leaders—the more time, the better. They, too, need opportunities to evaluate these potential candidates over an extended period. The result would be more informed choices when selecting a new CEO.

BREAK POINT

A survey of directors revealed they spend less time working with emerging leaders than on any other of their key duties. Ram Charan, author of *Boards That Deliver,* called that neglect "simply inexcusable" in an article in the *Harvard Business Review,* going on to say "organizations should be ready with a clear view of current and future needs and with carefully tended pools of candidates."

Boards should regularly review the top 20 candidates in the CEO pipeline, says Charan. At a minimum, they should devote two full sessions a year to thorough evaluations of at least five top candidates for CEO. And that's before the job is vacant.

So get your board members connected with your high-potentials. It will do them all good.

Mentoring Rising Stars

Mentors. Who needs them? Almost everybody, it seems. Read the biography of almost any contemporary leader and there's a reference to the college professor, military commander, or early boss who served as an example of leadership.

Every model of leadership development I've looked at recommends mentoring by a more-experienced leader, even though some authors lament the fact that not all mentors are created equal. The only people who don't get mentors are those who have already risen to the top. And a lot of *them* wish they had a mentor, or at least a trusted confidante.

Those who were mentored, mentor back. A report by the non-profit organization Catalyst found that high-potential talent who benefited from mentoring, coaching, or some other helping hand are more likely to extend their own hands to the next generation. More women than men (65 percent versus 56 percent) make the effort, and women are much more likely to develop women (73 percent) than men (30 percent).

Developing the Soft Skills

The mentor-protégé relationship is a two-way street. The value to the protégé is guidance, reassurance, and sometimes a shoulder to whine on. The mentor, meanwhile, develops his or her own interpersonal skills. Graduate business schools offer mentoring programs to take advantage of that peer-to-peer learning.

Participants in Stanford University's Arbuckle Leadership Fellows program are "learning how to be leaders who can develop others through coaching and mentoring." Second-year MBA candidates, in consultation with master coaches, spend two quarters mentoring their first-year MBA peers.

The program obviously benefits the first-year students but is actually aimed at developing the decision-making abilities of the older students. By developing their "strategies and tactics" for mentoring (who knew there were strategies and tactics for mentoring?), the future leaders are preparing to develop their own future employees. The process also hones the mentors' analytical skills and their ability to communicate.

The good old days of a cup of coffee in the lunchroom are so over! I may be chuckling, but the programs at Stanford and other universities underscore the importance of those elusive capabilities that seem to develop best with maturity—or mentoring.

Many leaders embrace the responsibility for developing others and, in fact, define themselves as leaders by the very fact that they are willing to bring others along the leadership path. These leaders adhere to the principle expressed in *Strengths-Based Leadership*, by authors Tom Rath and Barry Conchie.

"Unless you can, on command, write down a list of the people you have developed," wrote Rath and Conchie, "you may just be in a leadership position by accident."

Legendary University of Tennessee basketball coach Pat Summitt put it this way: "It's what you learn after you know it all that counts the most." She might have added that what you learn doesn't count for much until you pass it on.

Index

Symbols

"The 100 Best Companies to Work For" (*Fortune Magazine*), 63

A

Aberdeen Group's 2010 Strategic Workforce Planning survey, 61
acceptance of criticism, 42-43
achievement, advancement and growth, 83
actions of leaders, 4
  measurable results, 7
  pass/fail conditions, 6-7
  subtle techniques, 5
activation (motivation), 80
active listening, 44-45
adaptive thinking, 129-130
advancement and growth, 83
alignment, change management, 48
allies, coalition, 50
Amelio, Gilbert, 35
AmerenUE, 37

Arbuckle Leadership Fellows program (Stanford), 133
Aronson, Elliot, 111
The Art of Chaordic Leadership, 93
The Arts of Leadership, 116
assessing assets, change management, 57
assets
  assessing/assigning for change, 57
  employees, 60-61
assigning assets, change management, 57
attitude, change management, 51-52
attributes
  future leaders, 131
  team leadership, 116-117
audience awareness, communication strategies, 33
authentic communication, 36
  acceptance of criticism, 42-43
  blogging, 37-38
  call-and-response activity, 40-41
  collaborative approach, 43-44

empowering supervisors,
39-40
face-to-face meetings,
38-39
feedback, 41-42
personal commitment to
cause, 37
authoritarianism, 96-97
autonomy, 81-82

B

"The Bat Computer" (Intuit),
65
behavioral changes, 51-52
behavioral interviews, 71
behavioral tests, 70
Bell, Robert, 106
"best-in-class" companies, 61
*Beyond Paper or Plastic—
8 Items or Less to Remarkable
Service*, 107
blogging, authentic communication, 37-38
board of directors, evaluation
of future leaders, 132
Boards That Deliver, 130
body language, 39
BP oil spill, 110-112
Bratton, John, 113
Bratton, Police Commissioner
William, 55
bridging gaps, personality
types, 18
communication, 20-21
deciphering messages,
19-20
Byrne, Mayor Jane, 50

C

call-and-response activity,
authentic communication,
40-41
Campbell Soup Co., 94
candidate screens, hiring
employees, 68
core competencies, 72-73
interviews, 71-72
prehire testing, 70
references, 69-70
Chambers, John, 37
change management, 47
alignment, 48
assessing/assigning assets,
57
breaking goals into attainable steps, 54-56
creativity, 56-57
influencers, 48
behavioral/attitude
change, 51-52
differences one person
can make, 49
embracing opposition,
50-51
rewarding valued results,
53-54
strategy and effect,
52-53
making most of resources,
56
chaordic management (Hock),
92-93
authoritarianism, 96-97
composure in a crisis, 96
creating positive environments, 94-95

focus on employee
strengths, 97-98
characteristics, leaders, 2-4
Charan, Ram, 130
"circle organization" (Harley-
Davidson), 124
coalition of allies, 50
Colgate-Palmolive, 126
collaborative leadership, 10,
43-44
combining personality types,
26-27
Commanders Handbook, 31
commitment
authentic communication,
37
increase after employee
input, 82
communication
hiring employees, 67-68
personality types, 20-26
strategies, 30
active listening, 44-45
authentic communica-
tion, 36-44
cultural awareness,
32-34
executive team, 35
principles, 31-32
rank-and-file employees,
35
supervisors, 35
company-wide team-based
structure, 120-121
compensation, job enrichment,
101
complementary abilities, team
leadership, 118

Compliant Analytics, 17-18,
25-26
Conant, Douglas, 95
Conchie, Barry, 134
constructive dissent, 113, 117
core competencies, 60-61,
72-73
creativity, change management, 56-57
Creech, General Wilbur
change management, 52
charge of TAC, 4-7
criticism, authentic communication, 42-43
cultural awareness, strategic
communication, 32-34
culture of recruitment (hiring
employees), 60
employees as talent scouts,
62-63
identifying best sources of
candidates, 64-65
liabilities and assets, 60-61
social media, 65
touting brand as great
employer, 63-64

D

deciphering messages, bridging gaps between personality
types, 19-20
destructive consent, 113
development of relationships,
67-68
dissatisfiers (Herzberg), 101

diversity, hiring employees, 66-67
DiversityInc, 37
dysfunctional teams, 120

E

Economist Intelligence Unit, 38
Eisenhower, President Dwight D., 3, 91
Eitel, Maria, 49
employees
    engagement in meaningful work, 79
        advancement and growth, 83
        business results, 89
        Gallup Q12, 86-87
        input multiplies commitment, 82
        praise, 85-86
        recognition/reward, 83-85
        responsibility/autonomy, 81-82
        versus motivation, 80-81
        work and well-being survey, 87-89
    focus on strengths, 97-98
    future leaders, 125
        adaptive thinking, 129-130
        attributes, 131
        board of directors, 132
        emerging talent, 127
        high-potential candidates, 127-128

mentors, 132-134
succession planning, 130-131
training programs, 128-129
hiring, 59
    culture of recruitment, 60-65
    development of relationships, 67-68
    diversity, 66-67
    on-boarding new employees, 73-76
    screening candidates, 68-73
job enrichment, 99
    compensation, 101
    expertise, 100
    responsibility, 100
job satisfaction, 98-99
psychological contracts, 92-95
referral programs, 62-63
engaged employees, 79
    advancement and growth, 83
    business results, 89
    Gallup Q12, 86-87
    input multiplies commitment, 82
    praise, 85-86
    recognition/reward, 83-85
    responsibility/autonomy, 81-82
    versus motivated employees, 80-81
    work and well-being survey, 87-89

enrichment (job), 99
 compensation, 101
 expertise, 100
 responsibility, 100
Enron Corp., 112
Enterprise Rent-A-Car, 54
Enterprise Service Quality
 Index (ESQI), 54
environment, creating positive environments, 94-95
Ernst & Young, 63
ESQI (Enterprise Service
 Quality Index), 54
executive team, 35, 119-120
extroverts
 people-focused (Social
  Influencers), 15-16, 22-23
 task-oriented (Restless
  Drivers), 14-15, 22

F

face-to-face meetings, authentic communication, 38-39
Facebook, 65
facilitating change, 47
 alignment, 48
 assessing/assigning assets,
  57
 breaking goals into attainable steps, 54-56
 creativity, 56-57
 influencers, 48
  behavioral/attitude
   change, 51-52
  differences one person
   can make, 49

 embracing opposition,
  50-51
 rewarding valued results,
  53-54
 strategy and effect,
  52-53
 making most of resources,
  56
FedEx, 107
feedback, authentic communication, 41-42
Fogleman, General Ronald
 R., 5
followers
 mutual respect, 92-93
 positive environments,
  94-95
 relationships to leaders, 10
Ford, John, 9
Fortune Magazine, "The 100
 Best Companies to Work
 For," 63
future leaders, 125
 adaptive thinking, 129-130
 attributes, 131
 board of directors, 132
 emerging talent, 127
 high-potential candidates,
  127-128
 mentors, 132-134
 succession planning,
  130-131
 training programs, 128-129

G

Gallup Organization, 86-87
"The Girl Effect" (Nike
Foundation), 49
goals, breaking into attainable
steps, 54-56
Grint, Keith, 113, 116
growth and advancement, 83

H

Harley-Davidson, 51, 123-124
Hayward, Tony, 111
Herzberg, Dr. Frederick, 81,
98
Hewan, Behane, 49
hiring employees, 59
    culture of recruitment
        employees as talent
            scouts, 62-63
        identifying best sources
            of candidates, 64-65
        liabilities and assets,
            60-61
        social media, 65
        touting brand as great
            employer, 63-64
    development of
        relationships, 67-68
    diversity, 66-67
    on-boarding new
        employees, 73-76
    screening candidates, 68
        core competencies, 72-73
        interviews, 71-72
        prehire testing, 70
        references, 69-70

Hock, Dee, 66
    chaordic management,
        92-93
        authoritarianism, 96-97
        composure in a crisis, 96
        creating positive envi-
            ronments, 94-95
        focus on employee
            strengths, 97-98
hospitality, new employees, 74
hygiene factors (Herzberg),
    101

I

in-person communication,
    38-39
influencers, change manage-
    ment, 48
    behavioral/attitude change,
        51-52
    differences one person can
        make, 49
    embracing opposition,
        50-51
    rewarding valued results,
        53-54
    strategy and effect, 52-53
informal teams, 122-123
Infosys, 34
input (employees), 82
integrity, 3
intensity (motivation), 80
interviews, hiring employees,
    71-72
introverts
    people-focused (Steady
        Eddies), 16-17, 24-25

task-focused (Compliant
Analytics), 17-18, 25-26
Intuit, "The Bat Computer,"
65

J-K

job enrichment, 99
  compensation, 101
  expertise, 100
  responsibility, 100
job satisfaction, 98-99
Jobs, Steve, 105

Kim, W. Chan, 55

L

"laggard" companies, 61
Langer, Dr. Ellen J., 82
leaders
  actions over words, 4
    measurable results, 7
    pass/fail conditions, 6-7
    subtle techniques, 5
  change management, 47
    alignment, 48
    assessing/assigning
      assets, 57
    breaking goals into
      attainable steps, 54-56
    creativity, 56-57
    influencers, 48-54
    making most of
      resources, 56
  characteristics, 2-4

communication strategies,
30
  active listening, 44-45
  authentic communica-
    tion, 36-44
  cultural awareness,
    32-34
  executive team, 35
  principles, 31-32
  rank-and-file employees,
    35
  supervisors, 35
development, 125
  adaptive thinking,
    129-130
  attributes, 131
  board of directors, 132
  emerging talent, 127
  high-potential candi-
    dates, 127-128
  mentors, 132-134
  succession planning,
    130-131
  training programs,
    128-129
ownership of mistakes, 8-9,
104
  acknowledging failure,
    107-108
  compassionate responses,
    106-107
  lessons learned, 105
  organization first,
    108-109
  setting expectations,
    105-106
  strategies that maximize
    damage, 109-114

personalities, 12-13
  bridging gaps, 18-21
  combination of styles,
    26-27
  communication strate-
    gies, 21-26
  Compliant Analytics,
    17-18
  Restless Drivers, 14-15
  Social Influencers, 15-16
  Steady Eddies, 16-17
positive, 91
  authoritarianism, 96-97
  composure in a crisis, 96
  creating positive envi-
    ronments, 94-95
  focus on employee
    strengths, 97-98
  job enrichment, 99-101
  job satisfaction, 98-99
  mutual respect, 92-93
  relationships to followers,
    10
  value of relationships, 7-8
liabilities (positions), 60-61
listening
  active listening, 44-45
  authentic communication,
    41-42
Lombardi, Vince, 78

M

management, change, 47
  alignment, 48
  assessing/assigning assets,
    57
  breaking goals into attain-
    able steps, 54-56
  creativity, 56-57
  influencers, 48-54
  making most of resources,
    56
Marston, William Mouton, 12
Mauborgne, Reness, 55
meaningful work, 10, 78
  employee engagement, 79
  advancement and
    growth, 83
  business results, 89
  Gallup Q12, 86-87
  input multiplies
    commitment, 82
  praise, 85-86
  recognition/reward,
    83-85
  responsibility/autonomy,
    81-82
  versus motivation, 80-81
  work and well-being
    survey, 87-89
measurable results, Creech
  leadership, 7
mentors, future leaders,
  132-134
mission, 2-4
mistakes, ownership, 8-9, 104
  acknowledging failure,
    107-108
  compassionate responses,
    106-107
  lessons learned, 105
  organization first, 108-109
  setting expectations,
    105-106

strategies that maximize
damage, 109-114
Mistakes Were Made (but Not by Me), 111
Mister Roberts (film), 9-10
motivation
achievement, 83
recognition, 83-86
responsibility, 81-82
versus engagement, 80-81
mutual respect, 92-93

N-O

Nelson, Debra L., 113
Nike Foundation, "The Girl Effect," 49

on-boarding new employees, 73-76
on-the-job training, 75
ONA (Organizational Network Analysis), 122
opposition, embracing, 50-51
Organizational Leadership, 113
Organizational Network Analysis (ONA), 122
orientation, new employees, 74
ownership of mistakes, 8-9, 104
acknowledging failure, 107-108
compassionate responses, 106-107
lessons learned, 105
organization first, 108-109

setting expectations, 105-106
strategies that maximize damage, 109-114

P-Q

Parks, Rosa, 1
pass/fail conditions (Creech), 6-7
Paterno, Joe, 110
people-focused extroverts (Social Influencers), 15-16, 22-23
people-focused introverts (Steady Eddies), 16-17, 24-25
persistence (motivation), 80
personalities, 12-13
bridging gaps, 18
communication, 20-21
deciphering messages, 19-20
combination of styles, 26-27
communication strategies, 21
Compliant Analytics, 25-26
Restless Drivers, 22
Social Influencers, 22-23
Steady Eddies, 24-25
Compliant Analytics, 17-18
Restless Drivers, 14-15
Social Influencers, 15-16
Steady Eddies, 16-17
personnel. *See* employees
positive environments, 94-95

positive feedback, 84
positive leaders, 91
    authoritarianism, 96-97
    composure in a crisis, 96
    creating positive environ-
        ments, 94-95
    focus on employee
        strengths, 97-98
    job enrichment, 99
        compensation, 101
        expertise, 100
        responsibility, 100
    job satisfaction, 98-99
    mutual respect, 92-93
praise, employees, 83-86
prehire testing, 70
principles, strategic communi-
    cation, 31-32
Principles of Strategic Com-
    munication Guide, 32
Proctor & Gamble, Talent
    Portfolio, 128
psychological contracts, 92-93
    authoritarianism, 96-97
    composure in a crisis, 96
    creating positive environ-
        ments, 94-95
    focus on employee
        strengths, 97-98
Purple Promise (FedEx), 107

Q12 survey (Gallup), 86-87
Quicken Loans, employee
    referral programs, 62-63

R

rank-and-file employees,
    strategic communication, 35
Rath, Tom, 134
Reach for the Summitt, 120
recognition, 83-85
recruitment culture, hiring
    employees, 60
    employees as talent scouts,
        62-63
    identifying best sources of
        candidates, 64-65
    liabilities and assets, 60-61
    social media, 65
    touting brand as great
        employer, 63-64
references, hiring employees,
    69-70
referral programs (employee),
    62-63
relationships
    hiring employees, 67-68
    leaders and followers, 10
    psychological contracts,
        92-93
    team leadership, 116-117
    values, 7-8
resources, change manage-
    ment, 56
respect, 92-93
responsibility, 81-82, 100
Restless Drivers, communica-
    tion strategies, 14-15, 22
reward system
    change management, 53-54
    meaningful work, 83-85

S

screening candidates, hiring
employees, 68
  core competencies, 72-73
  interviews, 71-72
  prehire testing, 70
  references, 69-70
Shackleton, Ernest, 104
shared governance, 121
Small Unit Leadership Handbook, 126
Smith, Fred, 107
Social Influencers, 15-16, 22-25
social media, 65
Sodexo, 66
Sottman, Dr. John, 84
staff. *See* employees
Stavridis, Admiral James, 31
Steady Eddies, 16-17
strategies
  change management, 52-53
  communication, 30
    active listening, 44-45
    authentic communication, 36-44
    cultural awareness, 32-34
    executive team, 35
    personality types, 21-26
    principles, 31-32
    rank-and-file employees, 35
    supervisors, 35
Strengths-Based Leadership, 134
succession planning, 130-131
Summitt, Pat, 120

supervisors
  authentic communication, 39-40
  strategic communication, 35

T

TAC (Tactical Air Command), General Wilbur Creech, 4-7, 52
Talent Portfolio (Proctor & Gamble), 128
talent scouts, 62-63
task-focused introverts (Compliant Analytics), 17-18, 25-26
task-oriented extroverts (Restless Drivers), 14-15, 22
Tavris, Carol, 111
team leadership, 115
  common attributes among leaders, 116-117
  company-wide team-based structure, 120-121
  complementary abilities, 118
  constructive dissent, 117
  dysfunctional teams, 120
  executive team, 119-120
  filling the gaps, 118
  Harley-Davidson, 123-124
  informal teams, 122-123
testing potential employees, 70
"Tipping Point Leadership" article, 55

training programs, 128-129
traits of leaders, 2-4
Truman, President Harry S., 2

U-V

values, 2-4
Visconti, Luke, 37
vision, 2-4
Voss, Tom, 37
vulnerability, authentic
  communication, 36

W-X-Y-Z

Wondie, Ato Tesfahun, 49
work and well-being survey,
  87-89
work motivators (Herzberg),
  98